KT-521-810

MODERN EDUCATION SERIES

SUMMERHILL: FOR AND AGAINST

ANGUS AND ROBERTSON

373 LAW

First published in the British Commonwealth in 1973 by
ANGUS AND ROBERTSON (PUBLISHERS) PTY LTD
102 Glover Street, Cremorne, Sydney
2 Fisher Street, London
107 Elizabeth Street, Melbourne
167 Queen Street, Brisbane
89 Anson Road, Singapore

First published in the United States of America in 1970

National Library of Australia
card number and ISBN
hard bound edition 0 207 12633 x
limp bound edition 0 207 12634 8

Registered in Australia for transmission by post as a book

PRINTED IN AUSTRALIA BY
JOHN SANDS PTY. LTD. HALSTEAD PRESS DIVISION

Contents

PUBLISHERS' INTRODUCTION TO THE
AMERICAN EDITION

When *Summerhill: A Radical Approach to Child Rearing* was announced in the United States in 1960, not a single bookseller in the country was willing to place an advance order for even one copy of the book, for A. S. Neill was practically unknown. True, he had lectured at the Rand School for Social Research in the early 1950's, but the handful who had heard him, however much impressed, were not sufficiently influential to establish a cult or a following of any dimension.

Now, some ten years later, Neill's book *Summerhill* is required reading in at least 600 American university courses. And the number is constantly growing. During the calendar year of 1969, the sale of the book exceeded 200,000 copies, an increase of 100% over 1968. In fact, the interest in Summerhill has now become world-wide; there are now translations in French, German, Italian, Spanish, Portuguese, Japanese, Hebrew, Finnish, Norwegian, and Danish.

What accounts for the growing interest in this book ten years after publication? Most certainly, Neill's ideas have stirred up an enormous amount of controversy. His educational theories have, at one and the same time, been championed by some of America's leading thinkers and utterly derided by scholars and specialists of equal eminence. It is quite possible that in some classes where Summerhill is used as a text, the book is primarily used to show how far off a man can be in his thinking. But no matter how you read Neill, Summerhill is a springboard that will engender heated discussion, whether the situs of the discussion be the classroom or the drawing-room.

The polarity was evident from the start. When the book was

first published, a postcard was placed in the fly-leaf to solicit the opinion of the reader. More than 25% of these cards were returned —an unusual response, as any mail-order man will testify. But even more striking was the intensity of the feelings which these cards revealed. Many of the writers plainly stated that *Summerhill* was "the greatest book I've ever read," and "the most important influence in my life." On the other hand, I remember one woman who returned her copy for a refund on the ground that her husband had told her that either she or the book must get out of the house.

Because of the enormous interest in Neill's basic concepts I invited a number of leading thinkers to discuss his principles pro and con. The essays which comprise this book were contributed by writers who have achieved recognition in a number of disciplines. No viewpoints were barred; no limits were imposed.

As expected, the opinions in this book vary widely, Max Rafferty, California State Superintendent of Public Instruction, regards the atmosphere of Summerhill as utterly iniquitous. He writes, "I would as soon enroll a child of mine in a brothel as in Summerhill." On the other hand, John Culkin, Jesuit priest, regards Summerhill as "a holy place."

Summerhill: For and Against represents a fairly complete spectrum of present-day thinking about child training and education. If this book leads to a more thorough-going consideration of the problems, its goal will have been achieved.

HAROLD H. HART

A. S. Neill:
An Introduction

MAX LAWSON*

A. S. Neill has become a kind of Father Christmas figure of progressive education: his advice seems always kindly and the young
write him many letters. It is rather sad, however, that Neill is
treated as a guru particularly by those who may only know him
by hearsay or through the picture books that inevitably surround
a cult figure. Therefore is it good to see the appearance of such
a collection as *Summerhill: For and Against*; few educators are in
such need of being placed in perspective—not only because Neill is
the subject of much mindless adulation on the one hand and ill-
informed criticism on the other, but also because Neill is all too
readily assimilated, all too neatly pigeonholed into his "proper"
place in educational thought. After all, the argument runs, we
must have someone on the extreme edge of the spectrum of education to help us see our own position more clearly. Furthermore, the
argument persists, Neill's stress on freedom in education cannot
be totally ignored just as Quakers are still conceded to be Christ-
ians despite their insistence that Jesus spoke more about peace than
about the Trinity.

The furore about Neill's Summerhill—established in 1921—stems
from Neill's fifty year old practice of leaving his pupils free, of
endeavouring not to mould their characters. In the first decades
of the school's history Neill relied much on psycho-analytic methods for the disturbed children in his charge, but, when he attracted
pupils from parents who believed in his methods as such, Neill
dropped his psycho-analytically orientated sessions with pupils
(referred to as "private lessons") in favour of complete freedom.

* Max Lawson lectures in English at Sydney Teachers College. With
R. C. Petersen he wrote the book *Progressive Education: An Introduction*
published in this series.

Indeed Neill came to believe that "freedom alone will cure most delinquencies in a child".

Neill is by no means a highly original thinker; he himself has frequently acknowledged his indebtedness to others, particularly to Homer Lane, whose educational venture in self-government with "delinquent" children Neill once categorized as "a Christ-like experiment". Although Homer Lane's community, the little Commonwealth, was short lived, because it ran foul of officialdom, Neill nevertheless sees Lane's influence as being no less than "the beginning of child-centred education". In ascribing this position to Lane, Neill dismisses previously existing English progressive schools as being founded by people "who thought they knew what sort of school children ought to have". Furthermore, although such schools were improvements on existing ones they nevertheless conditioned their pupils, even if "in a kindly way". Although Lane was heavily indebted to Freud, Neill has stated that, "Lane's use of Freud was less important than the idea that children should be basically free".

Neill has persevered with this belief in freedom for over half a century, a faith whose consequences eventually broke the stamina of other men—including Lane. Despite lack of privacy at Summerhill and the constant demands made on Neill's time, he has shown a remarkable endurance in living up to his educational credo that "my life is one long give and it should be. We must give to the children". Neill adds a caveat that "it may be better to give than receive, but it is certainly more exhausting".

One of the commonest misconceptions about Neill is that he is aggressively anti-intellectual. Neill, the Scots dominie, is in fact a great reader. (He doesn't spend all his time—as rumour would have it—repairing his property from the onslaught of his vandal pupils.) Indeed if all teachers, particularly Neill's fellow head-masters, had spent as much time studying and reading in education and related fields we may well have had an educational revolution on our hands greater than the dreams of some of those who wish to "deschool society".

In his books of the 1920s Neill referred his readers to many of the progressive educators of the period (Neill has stated that he "can't stand the word 'progressive', preferring pioneer"—though he uses it nevertheless): Homer Lane, Dewey, Edmond Holmes, Caldwell Cook, Montessori. In this period, however, books on psychology outweigh those on education—standard works of Freud, Jung and Adler being cited. Yet Neill did not remain with the gods of the old dispensation: Neill's most recent book, *Talking of Summerhill*, refers, for example, to Wilhelm Reich, Krishnamurti, Paul Goodman, Erich Fromm and Melanie Klein, even if there are still more references to Homer Lane than other educators or psychologists. Such emphasis is understandable when it is recalled that Neill placed Homer Lane "as a greater educator than the 'Big Four'—Rousseau, Pestalozzi, Froebel and Montessori".

Of all the educators that Neill refers to he is perhaps most hard on Montessori. Having been so used to noise at Summerhill, Neill referred to the children he saw working silently and individually with the self-instructing Montessori apparatus as "hives of buzzless bees". Of Montessori herself Neill has suggested that Montessori's initial success was partly because of the fact that "she never made a joke, always being the dignified moral model teacher".

Yet on the other hand Neill's own lack of stodginess, his easy journalistic style, his persistence in writing books on education that are not only easy to read but have jokes in them—all these factors have made Neill a model teacher for many students of education.

Only the commonplace never attracts criticism and Neill has been as much reviled as he has been praised. It is to the credit of most of the contributors of *Summerhill: For and Against* that they take the fundamental issues Neill raises seriously—far too often discussion of Summerhill never gets beyond peripheral matters such as why Summerhill students are allowed to wear pullovers and jeans rather than other kinds of school uniform. It is a pity such matters are often emphasized at the expense of Summerhill's real achievements such as keeping the tradition of self-government in education alive. The importance Neill attaches to self-government at Summerhill is shown in his belief that "if all schools had real self-government—not the brand that makes the pupils do the dirty work for the teachers—a new generation would face life with a high standard of public morality".

On a lighter note, Neill must be somewhat amused by a book such as *Summerhill: For and Against*; it is not every day that a headmaster has a State Superintendent of Schools say that he would rather send his children to a brothel than Summerhill and on the other hand a Jesuit priest state that Summerhill is a "holy place".

Blame Neill. His insistence on freedom, self-government, leaving the child alone, makes *Summerhill: For and Against* necessary. In such matters no teacher or student can afford to be neutral. Let Neill have the last word: "If at last I become a senile raving man of 90 that fact will not alter the fact that I founded Summerhill".

Max Rafferty, California State Superintendent of Public Instruction, has more schools and more school children under his supervision than any other man in the country. Dr. Rafferty is one of the most talked of figures in American education today. His syndicated column on education is currently featured in more than 50 newspapers from coast to coast.

In 1962, he wrote a bestseller on education entitled SUFFER, LITTLE CHILDREN.

A native of New Orleans, Dr. Rafferty, now 52, is the holder of honorary doctoral degrees from Lincoln University and Brigham Young University.

Max Rafferty

Summerhill is old hat, you know. Not new. Not revolutionary. Not even shocking.

It's hard to pinpoint the first educational quack. I suppose the line of frauds goes back well beyond Jean-Jacques Rousseau, but that heartless mountebank will serve as a starting point.

Jean-Jacques was a real character. With an irresponsibility characteristic of his entire philosophy, he fathered several bastards and thoughtfully shunted them into foundling asylums for his more humdrum fellow-citizens to support. At various times he practiced voyeurism, exhibitionism, and masturbation with equally feverish enthusiasm, preserving himself from any legal unpleasantness by pleading softening of the brain. He fought viciously, if verbally, with every normal intellect in Europe, and died insane.

Rousseau spawned a frenetic theory of education which after two centuries of spasmodic laboring brought forth a by-blow in the form of A. S. Neill's neolithic version of the hallowed halls of academe: Summerhill. According to the confused Frenchman, education was running, jumping, shouting, doing as one pleased. The first impulses of nature are always right. Keep the child's mind idle as long as you can. And suchlike rot.

This sort of guff is as old as the human race. The child is a Noble Savage, needing only to be let alone in order to insure his intellectual salvation. Don't inhibit him. Never cross him, lest he develop horrid neuroses later on in life. The cave children of the Stone Age grew up happier, better adjusted, and less frustrated than do ours today, simply because they were in a blissful state of nature. So just leave the kids alone. They'll educate themselves.

Twaddle.

Schooling is not a natural process at all. It's highly artificial. No boy in his right mind ever wanted to study multiplication tables and historical dates when he could be out hunting rabbits or climbing trees. In the days when hunting and climbing contributed to the survival of *homo sapiens,* there was some sense in letting the kids do what comes naturally, but when man's future began to hang upon the systematic mastery of orderly subject matter, the primordial, happy-go-lucky, laissez-faire kind of learning had to go. Today it's part and parcel of whatever lost innocence we may ever have possessed. Long gone. A quaint anachronism.

Except at Summerhill.

The story of mankind is the rise of specialization with its highly artificial concomitants. Over the years, natural medicine gave way to anesthesia, antiseptics, and antibiotics. In the field of transportation, hiking sturdily along dim forest trails took a back seat to freeways, air routes, and eventually lunar orbits. And in the communications sector, old Stentor himself, brass lungs and all, couldn't compete today with radio and the telephone.

So it is with education. When writing was invented, "natural" education went down the drain of history. From then on, children were destined to learn artificially, just as men around the world were increasingly to live artificially. This is civilization—the name of the game. When Rousseau and his cave-dwelling modern imitators cry out against artificiality, they are in fact down on all fours, mopping and mowing, hurling twigs and dirt at civilization. For all civilization is artificial.

This brings us gently on to Summerhill.

Just as Rousseau was the engendering spirit of Romanticism two hundred years ago, so too is A. S. Neill the soul of Summerhill, if one can say this accurately of an institution which acknowledges neither soul nor God. Hear him intone his own hemi-decalog:

> *"The aim of education is to work joyfully and and find happiness."*
>
> *"Make the school fit the child."*
>
> *"The absence of fear is the finest thing that can happen to a child."*
>
> *"Lessons are optional. Children can go to them or stay away from them—for years if they want to."*

and

> *"Heterosexual play in childhood is the royal road to a healthy, balanced sex life."*

Every one of these Devil's Dictionary definitions is seductive, specious, and spurious. Allow me to demonstrate:

(1) *"The aim of education is to work joyfully and find happiness."*

No it isn't.

The aim of education is to give young people the intellectual tools which the race over the centuries has found indispensable in the pursuit of truth. Working joyfully, finding happiness, making a million dollars, trapping a sexually attractive mate—all these consummations are, I suppose, devoutly to be wished and have in fact occupied a considerable fraction of human interest and ingenuity down the ages. But none of them has much to do with the main goal of education, which is the equipping of the individual with the arsenal he will need throughout life in his combat against the forces of error. Happiness is a byproduct of education, not its be-all and its end-all. Education does not guarantee happiness. It merely enables one to be more discriminating in his quest for that elusive butterfly.

(2) *"Make the school fit the child."*

But will life in later years recast its iron imperatives to fit the individual? And isn't the school supposed to be, in the large, divine and comfortable words of the Gospel according to St. John Dewey, a microcosm of life, or at the very least a preparation for it?

If we deceive the child into thinking that life is going to adapt itself to him through all the vexing decades ahead, then surely we are lying to him in the most cynical and scoundrelly fashion. More, we are sowing the dragon's teeth of disillusion and defeat for every youngster who goes through his formative years swaddled in a cotton-batting environment of sweetness and light, only to have the ugly face of reality thrust suddenly into his own at the age of eighteen.

Sooner or later, a human being must come to an arrangement with the world about him. Either he adjusts to it, or by dint of personality, intelligence and force of will he shapes a small corner of it more closely to his heart's desire. In either case, he will be ill-fitted for the task if his teachers have convinced him since infancy that the universe is going to accommodate itself to him.

The school must meet individual needs and differences, true enough. It should help the child in every possible way to prepare himself for life in a world diked and plowed by two hundred generations of men past. The school should be just. It should be kindly. It should by all means be as interesting as possible. But it should not and it cannot "fit" every child.

Mr. Neill conceives the school as Proteus. It isn't. It's Atlas, holding up the centuries of human thought. Somehow the children of each generation must come to terms with the titan.

(3) *"The absence of fear is the finest thing that can happen to a child."*

In Heaven, yes. On our imperfect earth, certainly not. It's one of the worst things which could possibly happen to a child.

One wiser than Neill has said, "The fear of the Lord is the beginning of wisdom." This is one kind of fear, and a necessary one for sheer salvation's sake. On another level altogether, children should be taught to fear all sorts of earthly evils, from ant paste to sex perverts, if they are to grow up at all. Survival is the password here.

Assuredly the school cannot be an updated version of Dotheboys Hall, with assorted Squeers-instructors wielding terror weapons against panicked pupils. Fear as a motivation for learning is little better than no motivation at all. But fear, as an ingredient of existence, is as necessary for the survival of the species as is pain. Like pain, too, it has been a fellow traveller with man since the very beginning. When man ceases to be healthily afraid, he will be extinct.

The *unnecessary* fears are those which the schools should war against unceasingly. Ghosts, werewolves, witches, broken mirrors, skin a different color from our own—these chimeras should indeed be exorcised instructionally. On the other hand, live wires, drunken drivers, venereal disease, atomic fallout—fears of these all-too-actual menaces had better be encouraged by the schools, not discouraged, or presently there will be no more pupils to instruct, nor schools to instruct them, for that matter.

As we shall point out more than once, Mr. Neill's blithe penchant for striking generalizations in his little book betrays him into postures which only the charity of the reviewer keeps him from describing as those of a perfect ass. This is one of those times.

(4) *"Lessons are optional. Children can go to them or stay away from them—for years if they want to."*

Here the Progressive Education strand which runs through the tapestry of Summerhill comes on strongly.

Subject matter is relatively unimportant.

What is learned is less significant than *how* it is learned.

Cooperation and in-groupness and togetherness are the main objectives of instruction.

And I am the Maharajah of Mysore . . .

Let's exercise a little rudimentary logic. If the lessons are important, they should be taught to everyone, or somebody isn't getting what his parents are paying for. Conversely, if the lessons are unimportant, why bother with them at all? There is, of course, a third alternative: the lessons may be important for some, but not for all. In that case, why not diversify the lessons, so that all can profit from attending them?

Nowhere in the Summerhill philosophy does there seem to be the merest hint that children should learn to think and act in an orderly, disciplined manner. Nowhere is there even the insinuation that in this life, this world, this universe there are some things which are important to be learned, simply because—like Everest— they are there. If a child is to grow up saying and doing just as he pleases, there is precious little use in spending money on his tuition. He can do this sort of thing at home, free.

A school is not a health resort, nor a recreation center, nor a psychiatric clinic. It's a place where the massed wisdom of the ages is passed from one generation to the next, and where youngsters are taught to think in a logical and systematic fashion. A school where lessons are unimportant is a school where education itself has become irrelevant.

Is it, then, impossible to learn except in an institution?

By no means. Hundreds of great men have proved that a school is not essential to one's becoming truly learned. The experience of the great mass of humanity over the centuries, however, has demonstrated that the easiest, most efficient, and most economical way to learn is in organized classes, from trained instructors with assigned lessons.

A school, therefore, is taking money under false pretenses when it offers education without lessons. It can masquerade as a frolic in the park, a daisy-picking foray, or an experiment in free love, but it isn't a school unless it offers organized knowledge in some systematic way.

And if it lets some of its immature charges amass the wisdom of the ages while it simultaneously permits others to go out and romp in the hay, it is simply short-changing kids who are too young to know the difference.

(5) *"Heterosexual play in childhood is the royal road to a healthy, balanced sex life."*

Note that Headmaster Neill never concerns himself with corny old ideas like good or evil. The concept of virginity leaves him not only cold, but convulsed with mocking merriment. Mutual masturbation, he admits, is quite often practiced by pupils under his genial supervision, and he gives the definite impression in his book that he wouldn't raise the slightest objection if his adolescent clients were to stage a love-in, a gang rape, or a Black Mass with Neill himself presiding as Master of the Revels, for that matter.

It seems superfluous to point out that a child who is taught in school that premarital sex is perfectly jolly, comfy and gung-ho is apt to continue to practice it in all its ramifications when he gets to be an adult. And since Western civilization is based very largely upon monogamy and the family unit, Summerhill is obviously not only uncivilized but also anti-civilized.

This is perhaps the understatement of the decade. Speaking as dispassionately as possible but with complete sincerity, I would as soon enroll a child of mine in a brothel as in Summerhill. I know of no research which indicates that encouraging uninhibited sexual activity in childhood does anything to produce a sexually decent and happy adult. Neither does indiscriminate sexual experimentation at an early age impel the individual in later life toward an avoidance of sexual immorality. It would make as much sense for Mr. Neill to teach his little friends to sandpaper their finger ends and manipulate tumblers in the dark, and then to claim that this would induce in them a healthier attitude toward safecracking. What the unkempt and sometimes terrifying generation of to-morrow quite obviously needs are more inhibitions, not fewer.

Judging from the amount of space the author devotes to the topic in his book, Summerhill must be the sexiest spot since Sybaris. This rather nasty facet of Mr. Neill's flawed diamond reminds me irresistibly of the comment Bentley made upon the publication of Pope's translation of the Iliad, "A fine poem, Mr. Pope, but you must not call it Homer."

Summerhill may be a very pretty and permissive piece of phallic paganism, Mr. Neill, but you mustn't call it school. You really mustn't.

❁   ❁   ❁   ❁

If time but permitted, a coldly logical analysis of a few other direct quotations from Mr. Neill would prove not only illuminating but positively enticing.

> "*Discipline creates fear, and fear creates hostility.*"
> "*Summerhill pupils don't stand room inspection, and no one picks up after them.*"
> "*My staff and I have a hearty hatred of all examinations.*"

and most revealingly

"Summerhill is a difficult place in which to study."

But alas! Temptation must be spurned by the resolute reviewer, no matter how juicily it may offer itself, and peripheral opportunities must be sternly set aside in order that we may come grimly to grips with the main body of Neill's folly.

It's not really the headmaster's statement of principles which bothers me so much as it is his obvious hypocrisy. He wrote his book apparently to prove that the example set by Summerhill can and should be practiced by education in general. Yet he admits that he takes only the children of the well-to-do: "We have never been able to take the children of the very poor."

This, of course, makes Summerhill an exercise in aristocratic futility. In America, we educate everybody. True, we do it under certain difficulties, and the results, to say the least, are somewhat mixed. But we don't just teach the children of wealthy atheists, as Mr. Neill confesses he does. Neither are we able to limit luxuriously our enrollment to 70, and then to employ a staff of seven or more to instruct them. A pupil-teacher ratio of ten to one is a little rich for our Yankee blood. Our American ratio is more like 30 to one.

Just as an aside, almost *any* educational philosophy can be implemented with fair results if the school is able to supply one teacher for every ten pupils. With that kind of tutorial staffing and with above-average intellects to educate, Neill should be able to teach his kids to do everything except levitate.

In his book, he brags that Summerhill graduates succeed in later life. But how could they fail? With their background, their wealth, and their brains, they would probably have done well if they had been educated in the Himalayas, with yaks as instructors. The test of a school or of an educational philosophy is how well it educates *all* kinds of children—rich, poor, smart, stupid, black, white. When Summerhill starts doing this, I'll be glad to stop back for a second look.

Another detestably hypocritical posture is to be found in one of the beaming headmaster's more sordid little anecdotes:

"Some years ago, we had two pupils arrive at the same time: a boy of seventeen and a girl of sixteen. They fell in love with one another, and were always together. I met them one night and stopped them.

" 'I don't know what you two are doing,' I said, 'and morally I don't care, for it isn't a moral question at all. But economically I do care. If you, Kate, have a kid, my school will be ruined.' "

It doesn't matter one whit to Neill that the baby will be illegitimate. Like his bedraggled spiritual mentor, Rousseau, he would presumably clap the kid into an orphan asylum and forget about him. After all, what are the woes of one more miserable foundling compared to the joys of "let's-all-have-a-ball-and-to-hell-with-the-consequences"?

Nor does he worry about the chilling selfishness involved in premarital sex, the anguish guaranteed by sexual experimentation on the part of those least prepared to face the consequences, nor even the breakdown of our Western code of morality implicit in the spread of Neill's hedonism to the majority of the next generation.

No, he worries about none of these things. Morality be damned. Delinquency be hanged. Venereal disease? Pooh-pooh! The only thing which concerns him is whether his school will be ruined financially.

"Economically I do care . . ."

You'd better believe he does. Because his school is his livelihood, and if it begins to be a breeding ground for little bastards, even some of his probably incredulous and certainly incredible parents might come to have second thoughts and to pull their offspring out of this junior-grade Gomorrah. And this would hurt Neill's pocketbook.

Faugh! What kind of pandering Pied Piper have we here?

When Summerhill gets a student who is a crook, Neill tells him more ways to be a crook.

When a child smokes at Summerhill, as many do, Neill lets him. Never mind the ghastly threat of lung cancer looming somewhere up ahead. Live it up, kids. The present is the only time there is.

When mass sex play is indulged in by his charges, Neill smiles benevolently. After all, the kids like it, don't they? And shouldn't children be encouraged to do everything they like? He wants to assuage guilt feelings, he says. But as everyone realizes who reads the daily news, who watches television, or who dares to visit a college campus these days, the problem of the next generation is not too many guilt feelings, but too few.

A teacher who deliberately encourages vice in children who have been given into his care for good or ill, and who profits economically for so doing, is no teacher. Not in my book, anyway. He's an educational prostitute.

In my home state of California, some of us fighting under the banner of "Education in Depth" clashed shield to shield and helm to helm with Progressive Education years ago, and brought it crashing heavily to earth. Summerhill, half a world away, evokes memories of that old strife. For this is no wave of the future, this Fata Morgana which goes by the idyllic name of Summerhill. It is a return to old Rousseau, to the hoary cliches and the half-baked romanticism of the 18th century. It's a pastiche of the Isle of Boobies and Never-Never-Land, of Pantisocracy, and of "Lord of the Flies."

Summerhill is convinced that there are no absolutes, no eternal verities, no positive standards of good or evil. We who follow the standard of Education in Depth know that there are, and know that education exists to identify these lasting values and to seek after them as long as life itself shall last.

Summerhill stresses complete freedom in behavior as the main goal of the instructional process. Education in Depth holds that the teaching of organized, disciplined and systematic subject matter is the principal objective of the schools.

Summerhill feels that the curriculum should depend entirely upon the immediate interests of the individual. Education in Depth wants a curriculum to provide for the individual the tools and skills he needs to become a cultured and productive citizen.

Summerhill believes that education exists to make the individual joyful. Education in Depth exists to make him learned.

Summerhill advocates "experiencing" learning through as many sense avenues as practicable. Education in Depth thinks this is a ridiculous waste of precious time, and regards reading and recitative discussion as still the most effective and economical method of instruction.

Summerhill holds that the pupil should be encouraged to compete only with himself, or rather with his own previous best efforts. Education in Depth believes that the success of the individual in later life depends upon how well he is taught in school to hold his own in an increasingly competitive world.

However, let us let the English themselves have at least the next-to-the-last-word on what is essentially an English phenomenon. Here's what the Ministry of Education, with the masterful understatement typical of the island race, had to say about Summerhill a few years back:

> *"On the whole, the results of this system are unimpressive. It is true that the children work*

> *with a will and an interest that is most impressive, but their achievements are rather meager."*

and

> *"To have created a situation in which academic education of the most intelligent kind could flourish is an achievement, but in fact it is not flourishing and a great opportunity is thus being lost."*

I can only bow to the Ministry's ability to recognize a fraud when it sees one. If only the purblind parents who turn their younglings over to the perpetually permissive Mr. Neill would bother to read their own Ministry's report!

But the very last word belongs traditionally to the reviewer himself, and I herewith claim my rights. As I remarked ten years ago in "Suffer, Little Children:"

> *"The educator should approach his class not as the chemist appraises his retorts nor the astronomer his nebulae but rather as the conductor confronts his symphony orchestra. From the breathless whispering of the strings, from the clarion peals of the brass, from the muted thunder of the percussions, the conductor will weave the very fabric of great music, threaded throughout with the polychromatic strands of his own genius. Even so will the teacher evoke from the myriad experiences and abilities of his pupils the chords which, laced and interwoven with something of himself, will ring grandly in the harmony of life.*

*There is a mingling of moods, an elusive interplay
of spiritual counterpoint implicit in the teaching
process which marks the closest human approach
to the phenomenon of symbiosis. In its highest
form it approximates creation . . .*

*"This is an eternal verity. It has always been
true. It always will be. It had the same solid ring
of reality in the days of Pericles that it will have
for our remote descendants. We must train our
teachers as a sculptor is trained, not as a physi-
cist. They must think like poets, not like statis-
ticians. For they are dealing not with things like
the chemists, nor with bodies like the physicians,
nor yet with minds alone like the psychologists.
To them is reserved the splendid privilege of
fashioning and nurturing those coruscating and
iridescent entities called personalities, transient
as glancing sunbeams but more lasting than the
granite of our hills. It is at once the most precious
and most dangerous duty entrusted by mankind
to men."*

That's why Summerhill is a dirty joke. It degrades true learning
to the status of a disorganized orgy. It turns a teacher into a
sniggering projectionist of a stag movie. It transforms a school
into a cross between a beer garden and a boiler factory. It is a
caricature of education.

Things certainly are learned at Summerhill. Things are also
learned in pool halls, drag races, and discotheques. But we do not
call these places schools.

Herein lies Summerhill's twin sin against the Holy Ghost of
education. It lies, and it corrupts.

Worst of all, it does these things to children. I'll spare you the Biblical injunction about child harmers, millstones, and the depths of the sea. I think you will know what I mean. I think Mr. Neill will, too. And who knows? Scuba diving with weights about the neck may be his favorite sport. In which event the Hereafter may hold no terrors for him, after all.

Reverend John M. Culkin, S.J., is one of today's foremost exponents of multi-media communication and serves as Director of the Center for Understanding Media.

Ordained as a priest at Fordham University, John M. Culkin received his doctorate in education at Harvard University. He taught at Fordham University where he was active in the field of educational broadcasting. He was founder and chairman of the Young Peoples Film Festival, New York, and is affiliated with the National Center for School and College Television.

His articles on film study, instructional television, and educational innovation have appeared in scores of periodicals.

John M. Culkin

The entrance to the kingdom of heaven bears a simple inscription: "Children Only." It was commissioned by the one who said in Mark X, 15: "Unless you become as a little child, you will not enter the kingdom of heaven." In another place he added: "The kingdom of heaven is within you." These two quotes add up to a simple guide to integral humanity and interior fulfillment— you become yourself by becoming a little child.

This is not merely a clever or cute way of talking. It passes the pragmatic test. Four of the most creative people I know are Marshall McLuhan, Charles Eames, Federico Fellini, and Howard Gossage. They are all fiftyish and they all share the common characteristics of playfulness, joy, adventure and roguishness.

Regretfully, this simple evangelical ("good news", remember?) truth has been bathed in a backwash of sentimentality which has obscured and distorted its validity. And, being lazy, we have chosen to write off the truth of it rather than follow its clean wisdom in a literal and non-metaphorical sense.

Yesterday (August 23, 1969) I spent four lyrical hours with my friend, 21-month old Angelina Armstrong, by her green tent in Bolinas, California. During that time she exhibited a lovely repertoire of femininity, intelligence, charm, fun, ingenuity and inventiveness beyond anything available to me on the cocktail party circuit in New York, San Francisco, London, Rome, and Tokyo. I want to be like her when I grow up. I want her to be like her when she grows up.

The number of people who would agree with my hopes for Angelina and myself is probably not large. I know that Neill does. He has helped me to arrive at these hopes.

Although I have never visited Summerhill, I know that it is a holy place. *Summerhill* is a holy book—charged with wisdom, love, and all of love's attendant qualities:

> *"Love is patient, is kind; love feels no envy; love is never perverse or proud, never insolent; does not claim its rights, cannot be provoked, does not brood over an injury; takes no pleasure in wrong-doing, but rejoices at the victory of truth; sustains, believes, hopes, endures, to the last."*

This quote—I Corinthians 13, 4-9—beautifully sums up the spirit of Summerhill.

The educational critics have, of course, had their fun with *Summerhill*. Their terror of the idea is probably the most accurate measure of its validity. The eunuchs have always been afraid of life. Many critics from the official academic world read books with the idea of finding what is wrong with them. My more pragmatic colleagues from the world of commerce read books to find what is right with them. One idea is worth a thousand pages.

My current concerns are with big media and little children. Television is a very big medium and a three-year old is a very small child, so let's talk about their relation to each other. Many of today's children are in front of a television set short days after the cutting of their umbilical cord because parents find that "TV keeps them quiet." By the time today's American children start elementary school they have already seen several thousand hours of television. They have been to the moon, to assassinations, to commercials, to cartoons, to Vietnam, to lots of places. By the time they have graduated from secondary school some 12 years later, they will have spent 12,000 hours in the classroom and 15,000 hours watching television! These are merely the fat facts of the matter.

All of the conventional wisdom which for eons has considered the school beginner as a blank page or an empty bucket is now assuredly bankrupt as, by the way, it always was. Today's young people (up to 20) are the natural citizens, the first born of the total electronic age—they were born into a world where television was part of everyday living. Those of us who grew up before television are visitors to this electronic planet and should almost be required to show passports at its ports of disembarkation. This is not necessarily to say that young is good and old is bad. It is just to describe a fact of contemporary existence—a fact which has not existed in previous ages, a fact which may assist in understanding some of what is happening today. The conventional categories may be useful as a focus for moral indignation, but they hardly serve to illumine what is in the bellies of all of us today.

The schools provide a very convenient point of insertion for cultural thermometers. (One may choose either oral or anal insertion of the thermometer depending on the needs of the patient and the theories of the non-patient.) Today's students live in the total media environment. They are exposed, almost without protection, to the full barrage of the complete electronic surroundings. Then these fast-moving, over-stimulated people are dropped into the schools—the slowest moving institutions within our culture. The combination is made for explosion. The explosions are taking place with great regularity, and they will continue to escalate until the schools realize that they must begin with the students and not the curriculum, or the teachers, or the administration, or the testing system or any of the non-student elements of the educational environment. Schools are for students. Everything else is just a means to an end, to be used or not used depending on whether or not it will serve the growth of students.

All of this seems platitudinous enough until we examine what the schools did to most of us and are now doing to most students.

All of this is platitudinous enough until we read Neill and see what it really means to believe in the potential of human beings. "Summerhill" is the ideal name for the idea. It is warm, bright, and up. My schooling took place in regions which should have been called "Winter Valley" or "Blizzard Mines". There was no malice involved, and there were some very summerish moments and people; but the overall philosophy of the environment, the silent language of the situation, was one of distrust, rote performance, and passivity. I visit few schools today that are very different.

One measure of the upside-downness of contemporary education is in the allocation of funds. In the United States today it costs approximately $2,500 per year to educate a college age student, and $500 per year to educate a six-year old. Even the ladies at the laundry know that a six-year old is more important than a twenty-year old. Let's reverse the whole game and put our money where our insights are.

Or we might blow the whole educational establishment out of the water by initiating two simple steps: 1) Remove all compulsory educational attendance laws from the books; 2) Make a grant of $1,000 per year to each school age child to be spent for his schooling. There might be some fun in the neighborhood as students and their parents set about spending that money.

The new media have made today's students aware of what is happening in what they sometimes call "the real world." At their own peril, the schools ignore this involvement of the students with the wider context. If the schools remain mesmerized with their own tracking system, they become increasingly irrelevant to the world of the student. They deal in what Whitehead calls "inert ideas." In confronting without capitulating to the facts of the new media, the schools can both make the students intelligent consumers of television, film, radio, music, and print, and can help them to work actively in creating images and sounds of their own in these new languages.

The wisdom of Summerhill is exquisitely suited to the needs of the child of the electronic age. It begins with respect for and love for the child. All good communication does. Neill's concern for the total cognitive and affective growth of the child has never been easier to acknowledge than in our day when the gravitational pull of the electronic media is pulling us toward such wholeness, while the traditional institutions still stress the fragmented and compartmentalized style of life (or death?).

The Japanese have a word which may be useful—*Kokkoro*. It means the "general headquarters for heart and mind." They perceive it as one place and one state of being. Unfortunately our urban, literate culture has more often opted for the splits and distinctions between things. A blend of the big media, the small children, and the spirit of Summerhill may help us to glue ourselves back together.

Television is a privileged medium for reaching both three-year olds and their parents. It is obviously no substitute for the total environment and personal involvement of a Summerhill, but it can demonstrate and encourage the experience and wisdom of Summerhill.

There are three headings under which I group my own hopes for the education of children. They should be encouraged to develop:

1. *A Sense of Self.* The same Lord who said: "Let there be light" also said: "Let there be you." The creative invitation to each of us is: "Become who you are." The role of the teacher must be to nurture this delicate process by removing all obstacles to growth and by providing a context of love, respect, competence and strength.

2. *A Sense of Sense.* Students should be encouraged to discover within themselves their own sense of right and wrong, true and false. The interaction between individuals freely involved in such a personal probe then leads to the positive exploration of the limits of such personal rights in varying social contexts. The sense of sense also refers to the individual's feel for his own body and his senses. The best learners will be those who have tuned up their total sensorium.

3. *A Sense of Nonsense.* Naturally.

It has been nice reading and writing about Summerhill. As an aficionado of film and television and a believer in their reaching power, I now leave my typewriter to plan a documentary film on Summerhill.

Fred M. Hechinger, Education Editor of THE NEW YORK TIMES, *has been awarded the annual prize of the Education Writers Association on two separate occasions. He has twice been the recipient of the George Power Memorial Award, and has also won the Fairbanks Award, and has received honorary doctorates from Kenyon College, Bates College, Bard College, Knox College, Washington College, and Notre Dame University.*

Among a number of other books, Fred Hechinger is the author of AN ADVENTURE IN EDUCATION: CONNECTICUT POINTS THE WAY, THE BIG RED SCHOOLHOUSE, *and* TEEN-AGE TYRANNY. *He has been a frequent contributor to outstanding magazines of opinion, such as* HARPER'S *and* THE SATURDAY REVIEW, *where his lucid and incisive articles are accorded much attention.*

Fred M. Hechinger

Summerhill is not a school but a religion. That is why one can be intrigued by it—can even admire it—without being converted to it. To derive benefits from it for one's children requires religious faith in the efficacy of its myths. As with every religion, faith distilled into fanaticism can be dangerous. But there is so much essential goodness of intent and spirit in Summerhill that its doctrine may—in modified form—be most beneficial to ordinary parents who send their children to a variety of ordinary schools.

The underlying dogma of the Summerhill faith is that children, if not subjected to any adult pressures or influences, are perfect seeds that will turn into beings of predestined goodness. A.S. Neill actually goes beyond this when he says: "My view is that a child is innately wise and realistic. If left to himself without adult suggestion of any kind, he will develop as far as he is capable of developing."

This is not unlike the idea of Rousseau's Noble Savage, only presumably without the savagery. It is a difficult theory for parents to subscribe to when they have in fact experienced mean and contrary traits in their children; but Neill would (probably with much justification) dismiss such objections by pointing to the mean and contrary streaks in the parents and other adults and to the mean and contrary treatment to which the children have been subjected.

The holy writ of Summerhill says that if the mean and repressive influences could only be removed, the child would flower into a good adult according to his capacity. Whatever his accomplishments might turn out to be, he would be happy, and happiness is Summerhill's holy grail. It is not off in some distant promised land; it is attainable.

True to this belief, the original Summerhill therefore has been made into a place in which the mean and repressive influences have been removed, to the best human ability. It is not something that can be totally accomplished, any more than church or temple can be purged of human corruption and made into the original Eden; but it is fair to say that Summerhill has been startlingly successful in approaching its own ideal. Neill, by admitting that not all teachers nor even all children work out, and some have to be let go, defines the limitations of the experiment with characteristic honesty. But on the whole, Summerhill has created an oasis in which the children are left to develop without pressure and repression.

But even if it were not a religion and Neill its prophet and patron saint Summerhill would not be a school. It is really a family—an ideal family, to be sure, without overly possessive attachments—with an option to learn, but no compulsion to do so.

Size and arrangements alone make it a family rather than a school. It is very doubtful whether Summerhill, even given the funds and the facilities, could remain intact if it had many more than the 45 youngsters, subdivided into many smaller living and playing units.

It is more than doubtful—it is inconceivable—that Summerhill could exist without Neill. Whether one agrees or disagrees with him (and only the most computerized misanthrope could totally disagree with him) the fact is that he is a man of saintly strength and force. His intertwined belief in the child and the idea becomes, in the sweep of his eloquence, virtually irresistible. And this is so simply because all reservations are easily rejected by his conviction: it is the corruption of the world around, not any seed in body or soul, that corrupts the child. It is a conviction, unshakably held by Neill (without any shred of truculence), that can never be disproven. Unfortunately, in the face of continuing corruption, it cannot be proven either.

The rub is that—however some of the disciples and imitators are sure to dispute this—Summerhill cannot be reproduced. It is doubtful that even the original Summerhill will be able long to survive its founder. Indeed, the occasional playful exercise described by Neill in which he pretends that he has died and is succeeded by some dictatorial school master almost seems like a subconscious premonition. Neill's successor, of course, will not be a martinet or scoundrel, although he may seem so to the children, but he will at best be a disciple. Disciples rarely save any enterprise or idea.

But with or without Neill, Summerhill, not being a school, cannot be turned into the prototype of anything but an occasional small reproduction—private, selective, special.

This is inherently so because—as Neill makes unmistakably clear—the great majority of the world's parents do not believe in his basic concepts. They do not believe that children can be brought up without the customary restraints; that children can be groomed for a competitive world without competition in school; that children can be left to go about their growing up without being made to attend class or study certain subjects and learn certain skills.

As long as this is so, there is no way of setting up Summerhills for great numbers—or for any more than the occasional odd parents who march to Neill's drummer. Neill himself makes it quite clear that he cannot fight the realities outside. There is pathos in Neill's realization that, while he may write about what he feels is wrong with society and teach the children of the few who agree with him, if he tried to reform society by action, society would fight back. He even believes, perhaps a little too flamboyantly or pessimistically, that it would kill him "as a public danger."

"Hating compromise as I do, I have to compromise here, realizing that my primary job is not the reformation of society, but the bringing of happiness to some few children," he writes with disarming modesty.

And so, Summerhill remains, in his own words, "an island." (He would not even think of asking the local newspaper to publish success stories about his old pupils, and could you be more of an island in this age of the press agent, and expect to go into mass-production.)

Yet, despite its limitations as a model for mass-education, Summerhill is one of the world's most powerful ideas that is not likely ever to die. It has lived before Neill, although it has rarely been represented with such dynamic, charismatic power. It will outlast him—nuclear fission permitting—as long as men live and learn.

Parents who love their children should know about Summerhill. Even if they refuse to share Neill's total faith they should try to imagine how much happier their children might be if their natural childish drives, curiosities and creativity could be given their way.

Just as Freud opened the eyes of men and physicians to the terrible damage done by sterile repressions, those who bring up children need to question, day after day, whether many of the old restrictions and taboos are not in fact mental and physical chains which, though designed to shape them, actually weigh their children down and misshape their bodies and minds.

In an age when mothers worry about College Board test scores before their tots enter nursery school, the Summerhill contempt for the educational rat race—for the school that trains rather than liberates—is an antidote against a terrible pollution.

At a time of frantic affluence, the Summerhill contempt for educational upward mobility to material success is a reminder that parental ambition to shine through the accomplishments of one's children can be mental cruelty of tribal savagery.

To all but the most incorrigible reactionaries, it is clear that there is so much wrong with social and political values today that an affirmative appeal from the heart is a humanitarian service to all. Neill says:

"Most political newspapers are bristling with hate, hate all the time. Too many are socialistic because they hate the rich instead of loving the poor . . . All the Greek and math and history in the world will not help to make the home more loving, the child free from inhibitions, the parent free from neurosis . . . New generations must be given the chance to grow in freedom. The bestowal of freedom is the bestowal of love. And only love can save the world."

To Neill, the issue is simple, perhaps oversimplified in the view of some non-believers. He sees a civilization that is sick and unhappy, producing children who, being made unhappy, will grow into sick and oppressive adults. He is repelled by the ritual of stressing the negative—saying "don't" to children rather than "do;" relying on fear rather than love.

Unlike other reformers, Neill is not a man of bromides. Except when he lives at Summerhill, he is near despair, knowing that "the fight is an unequal one, for the haters control education, religion, the law, the armies, and the vile prisons."

To Neill, "it is a race between the believers in deadness and the believers in life." It is a race in which "no man dare remain neutral . . . the death side gives us the problem child; the life side will give us the healthy child."

Every parent and every teacher—whether he cares about the arrangements and the dogma of Summerhill—ought to carry this warning with him to the nursery and to the classroom.

I recommend Summerhill to parents and teachers—but not without misgivings. It is a religion based on love for, and understanding of, children; but it carries with it a religious mysticism that should not be accepted without critical analysis.

There is, in Neill himself, a strange streak of anti-intellectualism, almost a frantic rejection of all academic value judgments. Whatever the child likes, whatever makes him happy, is equal to any other enterprise. Bach equals Elvis Presley.

Neill can get upset about a ruined chisel but refuses to fuss about a book carelessly left in the rain "for books have little value for me."

This, I think, is a flaw that affects the Summerhill religion and the Neill philosophy. It claims to be non-coercive; but the model and the life style of those who teach do, in fact, coerce, however gently. The priorities of Summerhill are so non-intellectual as to place the book, the literary masterpiece, the evolution of thought at a disadvantage.

Neill is undoubtedly right in objecting—almost as much as to John Dewey's "learning by doing" reliance on the pragmatic consumer lesson—to the sugar-coated abomination of learning by playing or French without tears; but I am not convinced that the way to correct the subversion of honest play is to give it unlimited parity with work. Neither the history of man nor that of pedagogy has offered convincing proof that the child, if left without adult suggestion will (as Neill insists), "develop as far as he is capable of developing" by his own initiative.

Neill claims, and his disciples make an important point of it, that children who have the innate ability and wish to be scholars will be scholars, just as those who are only fit to sweep the streets will sweep the streets—and are likely, if left to their devices, to be happy street sweepers.

This, it seems to me, is an over-extension of the Freudian principle. It does not follow that men, merely by being free of sexual repressions, will lead happy lives—even only sexually—unless they are also positively guided into the proper use of their potential. While innate scholarly ability is essential to the development of scholars, it is not realistic to expect the wish to be a scholar to be present in every academically gifted child. Surely, the sampling of the delights and possibilities of scholarship—the function of good teaching, in contrast to the sterile or rote approach to learning—is part of the process. If repression and coercion are wrong, is not the absence of exposure, or sampling under expert guidance, equally deficient?

"Whether a school has or has not a special method for teaching long division is of no significance, for long division is of no importance except to those who *want* to learn it," says Neill. I find no logic in this. Only the rare—even odd—child is likely to want to learn long division, ever, unless he is given to understand what intellectual purpose it may ultimately serve. This is true of so much initial intellectual endeavor that it is very unlikely that intellectual progress—or the life of the mind—would get a fair shake under Summerhill auspices. Neill appears willing to sacrifice brain to heart.

Neill's criticism of the conventional teachers is that they lack "the power to subordinate thinking to feeling." He is distressed by any schooling that "goes on separating the head from the heart."

This is an immensely attractive concept. It is attractive, in part, for very sound reasons—because there is, in truth, so much heartless use of brain power. Much of the suffering in the world and in any community is caused by the highly intelligent who act without feeling and conscience. Much of what pretends to be government planning—particularly in the area of national defense—is based on computerized data, without concern for the consequences to humanity or human priorities.

But concern about the downgrading of the intellect and the excessive reliance on feelings and emotions is that, in the end, the

results tend to be just about equally damaging to the only con-
stituency that counts—people. The history of reforms is strewn
with wreckage caused by kindly emotions defeated by lack of
intellectual rigor.

This, too, is what worries me about the similarity between the
Summerhill ideology and the present student unrest. Nowhere
does the Summerhill dogma have as much appeal as among young
rebels who seek happiness in activism. It is in the revolutionary
occupation of buildings and the fellowship of the sit-in that youth
finds emotional satisfaction based on the subordination of brain
to emotion. Unfortunately, it also often seems to be an extension
of just the kind of playing to which Summerhill accords such a
key role. Yet, it is the playful, happiness-seeking campus revolution that is likely, not only to fragment and undermine the
academic community, but frustrate and, in the end, disappoint
and alienate those who seek concrete redress of just grievances.
To uplift the poor and the deprived requires more than heart and
sympathy; it calls for effective strategies of social and economic
reforms. Perhaps the greatest risk of heart without intellect is that
it is so easily fooled, and those in search of power inevitably know,
and ruthlessly exploit, this.

There is natural appeal, too, in Neill's report that, no matter
how long some youngsters might have decided to skip academic
preparation, they quickly make up for lost time when they suddenly decide to aim for the university admissions examinations.
This may offer some useful commentary on the nature of those
tests—and the excessive and long-range worry expended on them
traditionally by many parents and their children. On that score—
if Summerhill manages to question and perhaps demolish some
sterile myths—much is to be gained. But it does not answer my
concern that much latent talent remains undeveloped in the
process and that indeed the occasional decision to opt for the

climb up the academic ladder is even more likely to be made on the basis of irrational, extraneous influences than under the system of more conventional pressures.

Her Majesty's Inspectors, who incidentally approached Summerhill with a model of understanding that might well be studied by those who have power over school accreditation and standards in the United States, in the end could not suppress some honest, professional doubts.

"To have created a situation in which academic education of the most intelligent kind could flourish is an achievement; but in fact, it is not flourishing and a great opportunity is being lost," the inspectors said.

To Neill, this criticism meant that even the most sympathetic education officials could not completely "rise above their academic preoccupations" and that they overlooked the fact that the system does flourish when a child wants an academic education. The question on which, not unlike the inspectors, I part ways with Summerhill is whether tastes and wants need not be nourished, trained, acquired. I often feel that, had I been permitted to benefit a little more from the Neill philosophy in my schooling, I might have gained some of his facility with, and enjoyment of, the chisel and the rake. But I would not want to trade such tastes and wants for my greater concern with books. While I agree with his contempt for dessicated bookishness in the worst of traditional education, I cannot accept attitudes which, as a matter of experience and observation, give the non-intellectual drives a fast and clear track.

Summerhill is rightly opposed to fear as a pedagogical tool. But Neill admits that the search for approval is a strong human drive, and in the concern for lack of approval (even by Neill and the best, most saintly of his teachers) there is, of course, an element of fear.

The goal—and I think the Summerhill disciples might be persuaded to accept this revision of the absence-of-fear concept—
ought to be to teach children to consider the consequences of
their actions and inactions, and in the light of such considerations
to curb their desires for instant gratification. What this calls for,
however, is the abandonment of the search for immediate happiness in the hope of attaining greater happiness later—with lesser
risks of creating unhappiness in others. Whether this can be expected of children, without more direct guidance and restraints
than Summerhill admits (or without so much covert manipu-
lation that it would make dishonest men and women of the
faculty), seems to me highly questionable. Even if Neill, and an
occasional genius like him, can bring it off, this seems to me the
kind of success story that proves the exception rather than the rule.

There is a direct line from America's Progressive Education
Movement of the 1920's to Summerhill. But in reality, there is
nevertheless a fundamental difference. The old progressives believed fervently in what they thought of as life-adjustment education, and only the more radical among them also thought of the
school as an instrument of social change or even revolution.

Neill clearly does not want to adjust children to the corruptions
and sterile competition of a life that he sees around him. This is
to his credit. Simply to train people to play the game, whatever
it may be, and to aim for the jackpot under existing rules is surely
a perversion of the educational process. It is not adjustment to life
but to death-in-life, and I applaud Neill's refusal to have any part
in such an enterprise.

But not to bring up children to understand, and cope with, the
realities and the challenges of the competition "outside" is to
offer them little more than an escape into their islands of happiness, impotent either to adjust to existing realities or to change
them into better ones.

In the end, the impact of Summerhill is—as it ought to be—in the needs of the beholder. Much depends on the society in which the schools exist which Summerhill wants to reform. If it is true in Britain, for instance, as Neill indicated, that many babies are still subjected to the tyranny of a rigid feeding schedule, then the need to remove these irrational restraints from child care is great. Her Majesty's Inspectors may have been surprised (and, I hope, pleased) not to find youngsters at Summerhill jumping to attention as they entered the classroom; but most sensible American schools have long since abandoned this disruptive Teutonic ersatz respect.

At a time when permissiveness in the American home and school has often become a mindless exercise in the abolition of all value judgments and standards of conduct, the Summerhill lesson should be read with caution and discrimination; it should be read particularly with the clear understanding that Neill would never expect any part of his religion to work without an abiding faith in the joint enterprise—adults and children together—of the search for what is good and right and peaceful. He seeks, as a result of the removal of restraints, not orgiastic license but self-discipline.

Unless Summerhill is considered in such a light, it can be very potent poison, encouraging parents and teachers in a hands-off policy, without the compelling dedication and love and, even more important, the essential adult example of righteousness and—I hesitate to use the word because of its chronic abuse—goodness. Without these ingredients, the free-style approach is dynamite. It may well turn children (even if they are indeed Noble Savages, which I doubt) into Ignoble Savages when they grow up.

But taken with these cautions an infusion of Summerhill into the minds of those who rear or educate children and into educational institutions is an important antidote against the suspicions and rigidities that creep into the brains of adults and into the policies of schools.

I recoil when Neill says: "The child should not do anything until he comes to the opinion—his own opinion—that it should be done."

But then I realize that Neill and his handpicked staff intend to be molders of opinion, though they would deny this, by way of demonstrated love and understanding—and with the added caveat that nobody's freedom must interfere with anybody else's.

This is why I agree with Neill that the future of Summerhill itself is of little import, while the future of the Summerhill idea is "of the greatest importance to humanity." My reservations about it are comparable to those I hold about many religious faiths and rituals in whose moral and ethical foundations I urgently concur.

The author of many works on current topics, Ashley Montagu enjoys public renown and an esteemed reputation as one of the foremost anthropologists of our time. Perhaps Professor Montagu achieved his greatest prominence after the publication of his controversial book, THE NATURAL SUPERIORITY OF WOMEN, *His many works include* THE CULTURED MAN, HUMAN HEREDITY, THE HUMANIZATION OF MAN, THE HUMAN REVOLUTION, *and* THE AMERICAN WAY OF LIFE.

Born in London in 1905, Ashley Montagu received his Ph.D. from Columbia in 1937. He was Chairman of the Department of Anthropology at Rutgers University from 1941 to 1945, and served as Regents Professor at the University of California at Santa Barbara in 1962. He now resides at Princeton, New Jersey.

Ashley Montagu

The important thing about Summerhill is that the ideas that made and make it work helped a great many people to understand several essential truths. Among the most important of these truths are: (1) the necessity of love, (2) that the only healthy discipline is the discipline of self, self-discipline, (3) that freedom is a great responsibility; and that, (4) among other things, a good teacher teaches his children these specific truths, as well as teaching them how to teach themselves. Above all, Summerhill has made us understand that instead of requiring the child to fit himself to the requirements of school, the school should adapt itself to the requirements of the child.

I first encountered these ideas when, in the early twenties, I picked up, on a bookstall in London, Neill's delightful book *A Domine Dismissed*.[1] I suppose I have been a Summerhillian ever since. Most of the ideas set out in Summerhill, 43 years later, are to be found charmingly anticipated in *A Domine Dismissed.*

Writing from his experience as a schoolmaster in an elementary school in a small Scottish village, Neill tells the story, in the form of a diary, of his dismissal by the community and the events which followed. In a moving farewell scene, he says to the children:

> *"I don't suppose any of you understand why I am going away, but I'll try to tell you. I have been dismissed by your fathers and mothers. I haven't been a good teacher, they say; I have allowed you too much freedom. I have taken you out sketching and fishing and playing; I*

[1] *A Domine Dismissed*, London Herbert Jenkins, 1917.

> *have let you read what you liked, let you do what*
> *you liked. I haven't taught you enough. How*
> *many of you know the capital of Bolivia? You*
> *see, not one of you knows."*

One of the boys asks, "Please, sir, what is it?" And Neill answers, "I don't know myself, Jim."

And there we have the essential Neill: honest, rejecting the trivial and the inessential, and emphasizing freedom to develop one's own individuality.

"Freedom," writes Neill, in *A Domine Dismissed*, "allows a child to develop its own personality." And in the continuing words Neill sets forth what I consider to be his whole doctrine.

> *"If Jim Jackson, after being with me for two*
> *years, goes into an office and shirks all unpleasant*
> *duties, I hold that Jim is naturally devoid of grit.*
> *I allowed him to develop his own personality;*
> *and if he fails in life his personality is manifestly*
> *weak. If Macdonald can turn out a better worker*
> *than I can . . . and I deny that there is any evi-*
> *dence that he can . . . I contend that he has done*
> *so at the expense of a boy's individuality. He has*
> *formed something from without on the boy. That's*
> *not education. The word derives from the Latin*
> *'to lead forth.' Macdonald would have made Jim*
> *Jackson a warped youth; he would have Mac-*
> *donaldised him. I took the other way. I said to*
> *myself; 'This chap has something bright in him.*
> *What is it?" I offered him freedom and he showed*
> *me what he was—a good-natured, clever laddie*
> *with a delightful sense of the comic. I think that*

> *his line is humour; more than once have I told*
> *him that he has the makings of a great comedian*
> *in him."* [2]

Neill misetymologizes the Latin for *education,* but, then so does almost everyone else. The English word is not derived from the Latin *educere,* but from *educare,* which means to nourish, to cause to grow. It is, perhaps a minor point in Neill's case, for though he misetymologizes the word, he understands its true meaning better than most.

Of course, Neill is quite right. The continuing traditional methods of "education" have really nothing whatever to do with the functions and purposes of a genuine education, namely, to nourish and to cause the individual's uniqueness and creativity to grow. On the contrary, what traditional education for the most part succeeds in achieving is the frustration of the individual's uniqueness and creativity. This is customarily achieved by putting the child on an assembly-line in which, instead of being treated as the unique individual he is, he is dealt with as if he were exactly like everyone else. In the factories called schools the child is forced to engorge large quantities of rote-remembered facts, and then at certain calculated ceremonial ordeals called "examinations," he is required to disgorge these facts onto blank sheets of paper, thus leaving his mind blank forever thereafter.

Those who possess the highest disgorgative capacities are considered the elect to be most highly rewarded, and are immediately tagged the cleverest and the brightest, even though as a result of their school training they are only too often characterized by an inability both to think and to feel.

It is instruction that is the pervasive disorder of our so-called "educational system." Neill from the first made it clear that it was

[2] *A Domine Dismissed,* (pp. "9-10").

not so much what a child knew as what he *was* that most mattered to him—a view in which Neill remains in the minority, though he is not as alone in that view as he once was. As Neill puts it, the question for the teacher is: What am I aiming at? What is the goal of humanity? Most teachers, says Neill,

> *"start out with the assumption that human nature is bad; I start out with the realization that human nature is good. That is the real distinction between the disciplinarian and the believer in freedom."* [3]

Neill tried to bring out the good that was in his children, rather than misguidedly attempting to repress an evil that was not there. Evil was almost always brought into being by those who, in their efforts to repress an evil that was not there, confused the child.

Neill seems to have been influenced, and certainly encouraged, by the theories and practices of Homer T. Lane, an Anglo-American educator, who set up a "Little Commonwealth" in Dorset where so-called criminal children from the public courts were given self-government, and were turned, according to Neill, into excellent citizens.

"Schooling," writes Neill in his 1917 book, "is the beginning of the education we call life, and I want to make it as true to life as possible." A splendid ideal; but there are some who would claim that life isn't all beer and skittles, that life imposes very definite requirements that must be met whether one wishes to meet them or not, and that therefore, there ought to be a little less permissiveness and a little more externally imposed discipline in a proper school. Neill recognizes this but feels strongly that the in-

[3] *A Domine Dismissed*, p. 43.

dividual should not be required to be obedient to rules simply because they are rules, but rather that children should be taught how to distinguish between arbitrary rules and those rules that are sensible.

Neill holds that no child should be compelled to do anything unless he wants to. This may seem extremely overpermissive to some. Perhaps it is. But what Neill means is that no child should feel he is being compelled, but rather should feel that he *wants* to do what is required, that he is acting from internal compulsion. And that is what a good teacher can, in fact, accomplish. Nevertheless, I do think that Neill underemphasizes the importance of learning some things.

On the whole, I think Neill is right about the learning of grammar; Shakespeare, as he points out, probably knew none; and certainly lesser human beings require none in order to speak and write both soundly and elegantly. But to say that one *needs* no grammar is to miss the point that the learning of grammar can be a most exciting and creatively useful experience; for grammar constitutes the philosophy of a language, and can become an incomparably fascinating introduction to the manner in which a people thinks and feels and views the world. So, grammar, in my opinion, should be taught. Alas, it is seldom taught in the manner I have described, and this is what Neill rightly complained about in *A Domine Dismissed*.

But criticizable as our methods of teaching grammar continue to be, that is no reason for rejecting the teaching of grammar altogether. Certainly I agree with Neill that it is better not to waste time on the traditional method of teaching that subject; yet I would forcefully urge its teaching as a branch of linguistics because of the valuable insights grammar affords into the nature of language and communication. Not only that. The informed teaching of grammar in the right hands can become one of the best ways of introducing the student of any age to the nature and meaning of humanity. Like arithmetic, grammar used to be taught, and mostly still is, from the child's point of view as a form of low cunning devised by sadistic adults in order to make life miserable for innocent and defenseless children. As Neill wrote in his book of 1917, "You learned a lot of facts, but you never asked why?"

Neill's view of education has always been socialistic, in the best sense of that word: the function of education is to make humane, live, involved beings, and all else is secondary. Fear and punishment must be abolished; love and trust should be placed in their stead. Education should lead the child to think and feel for himself, giving him the faith in himself which will enable him to become an effective, concerned, and involved member of society.

I believe that Neill errs in overlooking or underemphasizing the importance of giving the child roots in the background of his culture and humanity. It would seem to me that this would be desirable in providing the child with the sort of referents from which he can wing his way to fulfillment and independence.

"A teacher is not," writes Neill, "an encyclopedia of facts." He is an enquirer, a guide to be consulted rather than a didacticist. In this view, Neill was many years ahead of his time. He still is, even though before he was born, there were teachers like Pestalozzi and others since, like Dewey. The number of teachers who view themselves as guides rather than as filling-stations is still pitifully small. Nevertheless, there has been a distinct but slow movement in that direction of the development of some of Neill's ideas as expressed in his best known book *Summerhill*.

Insofar as it is possible for anyone to arrive at his own ideas on any subject independently of the influence of other writers, I can confirm to the hilt from my own experience, as one who has passed through the hands of various kinds of teachers, the validity of Neill's fundamental educational principles. I have experienced, loving, unloving, and indifferent teachers; and I know what a substantive influence, a lifelong effect—each in their different ways—such teachers can have upon one. Such an observation should be trite. Unfortunately it is not. But however trite it may become, it will never lose its importance. As Pestalozzi remarked nearly two ceturies ago, it is only through love that one ever succeeds in teaching anyone anything. Other kinds of teachers are merely instructors, not educators.

A teacher should be, before everything else, one who cares for the student, is involved in his welfare, is nourishing, stimulating, and supporting; one who leads the student into the universe of the best that has been said, done, and thought in the world; and who helps the student to acquire those techniques and skills which will secondarily serve to implement his knowledge. A good teacher ministers to the unique needs and personality of each student, and enables that student to find and fulfill himself; he treats each student as an individual in his own right and encourages him to develop his own uniquenesses.

The direction of all education should be, in my view, toward creativity, for every individual from the moment of birth requires to be created as a human being. The process of creation should proceed in a manner that fits the requirements of the individual's uniqueness, so that he may be as optimally realized and fulfilled as possible. In this process, he should be taught how to teach himself, the process of self-creation.

Above and beyond all else, he should be taught to love, for this is the principal humanizer of the potential human being. Organization, growth, and development of the potentialities for being human is best accomplished through love, which is but another and better way of saying what E. L. Thorndike found experimentally and formulated as the principle of re-inforcement, namely, that the organism learns better under conditions of pleasure or reward than in the absence of these.

But Shakespeare was several centuries ahead of Thorndike, for he makes Tranio say, in *The Taming of the Shrew,*

> *No profit growes where is no pleasure ta'en:*
> *In brief, sir, study what you most affect.*

And this, indeed, is what Neill tried to accomplish for his children.

It is not only that the child needs to be loved, but that he requires to love others; that his very health depends upon his being loved. Indeed, the child's ability to learn to love others—for the ability to love, and the ability to work together with others, and the ability to serve—constitutes the very essence of mental health. One must live as if life and love were one.

In this respect, I would myself go much farther than Neill. While acting out the principle that one teaches love only by loving, I would teach students the theory and art of loving and living. I would ground them firmly in the scientific facts concerning the evolution and nature of love, in order to give them a firm and verifiable understanding of the bases upon which the necessity of loving behavior rests.

An additional meaning of the word *education* is "discipline." I feel in this regard, as many others have felt, that Neill is far too permissive in his relations with children—almost to the point of anarchy. I agree with Neill that the only discipline that matters is that which comes from within—self-discipline. But this is something one must learn; and certainly it is best learned within the experience of love. Indeed, love has a firmness and a discipline which nothing else can equal, for love clearly recognizes when something is undesirable or harmful to the welfare of the individual, and therefore love forbids such conduct. The genuinely loved child, though he may feel momentarily frustrated by the non-satisfaction of what he desires at some particular time, will readily accept the frustration of an act intended for his benefit; for he will know from his experience of those who love him, that they must sometimes frustrate him, and that everything they have done in the past—right and wrong—has been intended for his welfare.

In any event, a certain amount of frustration is inevitable; even a necessary part of growth and development; for every child must learn to postpone certain immediate satisfactions for long-term goals. One cannot have or do everything one wants to *when* one wants to. It takes a maturing self-discipline and experience to learn this, and apply the principle practically to the art of loving and living.

Children want their teachers to be loving toward them. That means firmness on the part of the teacher, and the freedom to say "No" to them as well as "Yes". Above all, children do not want adults—neither their teachers, nor their parents, nor any others, to be their friends, their "pals," their equals. They want the adults to be what they should be: mature persons, performing their required roles as guides, stimulators, encouragers, critics, teachers, lovers, and supporters—but *not* equals. The adults should be persons who give their charges roots and wings.

It is not friendship that is called for in the teacher-pupil relationship, but mutual reciprocity of involvement at progressively increasing levels of complexity, at the end of which friendship between equals will inevitably develop. Friendship is something to be earned, not a right that automatically falls to one. Love is, or should be, the birthright of every child. Love must always be unconditionally given—otherwise it is not love. Friendship is something that can grow only between equals. To pretend that children are their equals for adults is to confuse roles and expectations. Children have a right to expect more from adults than a spurious and disorienting equality. They have a right to expect the inequality which must inevitably exist between the experienced, the mature, and the inexperienced and the immature. Adults, by virtue of the fact that they should know and understand more than children, ought to be in a better position to serve as guides than the children themselves. Hence, there can be no question of equality between them, except where adults have failed to perform their roles adequately, and children have often been forced to fall back upon their own resources. The resourcefulness of children should, of course, be encouraged, but not so much as a response to the inadequacies of adults as a necessary and intrinsic part of the whole process of development and maturation. Thus, independence, trial and error, and that magnificent trait of every child—curiosity—should all be encouraged with the help and guidance of those who understand what it means to be a child.

Very simply, before anyone can undertake the education of anyone else, be it infant or child or adolescent or adult, he must first be an educated person himself—that is he must understand the nature of human nature, and he must understand what, at his particular stage of development, the individual in need requires. There are some persons who seem to possess this knowledge almost intuitively. A. S. Neill is undoubtedly one of those persons. Intuition constitutes a combination of sensitivity and quick intelligence; and here, once more, is a trait terribly neglected in the education of children.

The newborn baby is born with an already highly developed ability to pick up subliminal clues with speed and clearcut definition. This sensitivity is a trait which cries out for development. Unfortunately, this ability is one that is usually blunted as a consequence, not only of the inattention it receives, but also as a result of the lack of sensitivity which the child experiences at the hands of adults. Growth and development in intuitive powers can only be achieved by those who are sensitive to the needs of children.

At Summerhill Neill has, for the most part, had in his care children whose parents had failed them and who had become behavior problems. (For such children especially, Neill's methods could hardly be improved upon.) Children who have lost faith in others and in themselves, in most cases, have had that faith restored at Summerhill. Neill's is not a blind trust of the untrustworthy, but rather a measured realistic approach devoid of false expectations. Neill accepts children for what they are, without blaming them for not measuring up to what we have been told they ought to be.

Neill achieved his results through his perfect honesty with his children, and also through his ability to make children understand that the pose of unswerving rectitude that adults so often assume in the presence of the young is a sham. Adults only too often unreasonably expect children to be better than they are themselves. Neill points out that everyone errs; that one learns by trial and error, and that one should not make too much of the errors but should try to understand them, and not make a habit of them.

On occasion, Neill makes what seems to me a rather questionable statement as when he says that the child who wants to learn will do so no matter how he is taught. I find this statement to be more than doubtful, for surely it is well established through the experience of millions of children that a child's interest in any subject may be permanently destroyed by poor teaching. The manner in which that most elegant and beautiful of subjects, namely mathematics, has in the past been taught, and in many cases continues to be mistaught, constitutes a horrific example of the damage poor teachers have done to possible interest in the subject.

Contrary to Neill, I consider the *method* of teaching fundamental, for the method is the message. From this standpoint, what is most important is not *what* one teaches, but *how*. It is not the words so much as the music that conveys the message; and in this connection, the most important quality the good teacher has to offer his pupils is the gift of his own personality. This is, of course, where Neill himself has so eminently succeeded. He, however, seems to overlook the fact that the personality of the teacher is an essential part of the method.

In *Summerhill*, Neill himself forcefully remarks that "Learning in itself is not as important as personality and character"[4]. That is a statement that cannot be sufficiently underscored. There was a time when schools made it a principle purpose of their being to cultivate character in their students. *Character* is a word that has virtually completely fallen into disuse, and a concept which has been replaced by the huckster term *personality*. Roughly, I suppose, the distinction between *personality* and *character* could be made by saying that "personality" is what celebrities have, and "character" is what persons of integrity exhibit.

One of the most destructive traits of contemporary schools is what seems like a virtual dedication to the extinction of individuality and creativity in the child by treating him, among other things, as if he were a mere anonymous unit in an agglutinated mass of other similar anonymous units. The best thing that has happened for centuries on university campuses throughout the world is the current recognition of the attempt on the part of these so-called educational institutions to obliterate the individuality of their students, and the active revolt by contemporary students against continuation of that abuse. Students rightly claim an active role in determining how their educational institutions shall be conducted. It is interesting to note that Neill, from the very beginning,

[4] *Summerhill;* p. 6.

gave every student and every member of the staff an equal vote in determining the issues before the school at Summerhill's General School Meeting. I believe that Summerhill was one of the earliest schools to institute active student participation in the government of the school. It would seem that, at long last, some schools are beginning to follow that noteworthy example, even though some of the school authorities and some of the students involved may never have heard of Summerhill.

It is to be hoped that the future will see every educational institution governed by both its faculty and its students. I would myself be strongly in favor ot discontinuing both the trustees and the administration; and I would delegate the functions performed by these bodies to both faculty and students. Participation in the processes of one's own education, at every level, should constitute an essential part of the educational experience for the very cogent reason that such participation enables the student to organize his learning experiences in a very much more vital and involved manner than is ever remotely possible in a system in which he is treated as a mere counter. Neill's description of self-government at Summerhill is delicious.

Perhaps the greatest tribute that has ever been paid to Neill and to Summerhill is the Report of the British Government Inspectors on the school to the Ministry of Education. These inspectors fully recognized the merits of the school and the principles upon which it was conducted. Although they did not approve of everything they encountered at Neill's school, in substance they were most favorably impressed by everything they saw. Recognizing that Summerhill had always operated under most difficult financial conditions, Neill's achievement is all the more remarkable. That the inspectors were above all most impressed by Neill himself constitutes a remarkable tribute to the man.

Recently Emmanuel Bernstein reported his findings on 50 ex-

Louise Bates Ames helped to found the world-famous Gesell Institute of Child Development at Yale University. From 1950 through 1967, she was Director of Research at that institute.

Dr. Ames has co-authored many books which are to be found on the bookshelves of almost every mother, teacher, pediatrician and child psychologist in our land. Some of these works are: FIRST FIVE YEARS OF LIFE, INFANT AND CHILD AND THE CULTURE OF TODAY, THE CHILD FROM FIVE TO TEN, YOUTH — THE YEARS FROM TEN TO SIXTEEN.

She has written over 100 scientific articles and monographs on child development. Her syndicated newspaper column, PARENTS ASK, *began in 1951, and is still running.*

Louise Bates Ames

Summerhill is an infuriating book. It infuriated me when I first read it, and it infuriates me today. This is largely because A. S. Neill seems so dreadfully opinionated. Everything for him is black or white. It is also infuriating that though admittedly he has a warm, strong feeling of sympathy and even of super-identification with children—especially with bad, rebellious, non-conforming children—he seems to know so little about child behavior. I think it irritates many adults that Neill is so 100% against the conforming, regimented, law-abiding, and inevitably somewhat restrictive, world we live in. He is like a small bad boy who somehow or other, finding himself in a position of authority, throws out all the usual rules. His book and his school seem a continual, blatant, nose-thumbing at the society we live in. Bad as that society may be, it's hard to believe it's quite as bad as he says it is.

Throughout his book, Mr. Neill shouts out his hatred for authority. That is his privilege; but he fails to acknowledge that there are many children and adults who are not as resentful and not as hostile as he is, many who accept the fact that people in positions of authority demand, expect, and are reasonably entitled to certain privileges and prerequisites; and many who accept the fact that to live in a social world, one must give up—or at least modify—certain natural drives and wishes.

In spite of all this, I do have considerable respect—(respect which he would probably reject in advance since he does not believe that people should respect their elders) for Mr. Neill.

I respect his sincerity—there's nothing phony about him. I respect the consistency of his approach—children should in his opinion have virtually total freedom, and he is prepared to give it to them. I respect his obvious love for children; he really cares what happens to them. I respect the fact that he wants to see every child permitted to learn in a manner and in a setting which suits him. I respect the fact that he wants learning to be fun—not a stultifying bore—and be a challenge to the child and not an exercise in memorization.

I believe that Mr. Neill, whatever his basic theories, is a dedicated human being and a born educator. My guess is that had he chosen to follow some quite different educational road, he might have been equally as successful as he has been choosing the path of apparently complete freedom.

As the Inspector for the British government reported of Summerhill:

> *"The Head Master is a man of deep conviction and sincerity. His faith and patience must be inexhaustible. He has the rare power of being a strong personality without dominating. It is impossible to see him in his School without respecting him even if one disagrees with or even dislikes some of his ideas."*

One feels from reading his book that this statement is true, even without ever having met the man.

The chief impression I get in reading *Summerhill* is that Mr. Neill is a man who cannot bear restriction of any sort. He seems to have an almost pathological need to remove all customary bounds of discipline from the child, as well as an almost desperate need to identify himself with the rebelling child against parental or any other adult authority, including his own.

He objects wildly to almost any of the usual restrictions set up for civilized living: the restrictions which religion imposes; restrictions set up to govern sexual behavior; restrictions which people ordinarily impose to help the growing child fit comfortably into social living; restrictions which education, in the usual sense, customarily imposes. He seems to feel that regulation of any kind is harmful, until the young person grows into a stage where he spontaneously wishes to regulate himself.

Thus he states plainly:

> *"In order to succeed, we have to remove all discipline, all directions, all suggestions, all moral training . . . A child should obey only to satisfy the adult's need for power."*

Neill apparently has never gotten over his own boyhood rebellion. He has constructed a whole philosophy of education apparently based on this personal rebellion. This leads to questionable extremes. Thus he projects his own apparent inability to bear regulation to his pupils, and he assumes that they, too, naturally rebel against, will be harmed by any regulation imposed from without.

It seems to me that the man who encourages the boy who is breaking windows to break *more windows*—and even helps him to do that—is still a little boy who is still sticking out his tongue at authority, even when that authority is his own.

Love, presumably, conquers all according to Neill: "A loving environment without discipline will take care of most of the troubles of childhood."

All of this need not be labored; it appears to be the central point of Neill's philosophy, and is made clear on almost any page of his writing. How can happiness which, according to Neill, is the chief goal of living be achieved? "Abolish authority!" he answers.

Neill tries to render his notion of almost complete freedom more palatable to conventional people by drawing what he considers a strict line between freedom and license. He favors freedom. He disapproves of license. He defines the latter as "overextended freedom." A free child, according to him, can decide what he *doesn't* want to do, but that child cannot always decide what he *does* want to do. Thus the child can do what he chooses so long as it does not interfere with the freedom of somebody else. Neill admits that a child should respect the rights of others. It is a little hard to understand why the child should respect the *rights* of others when he is admonished not to respect those others: "To me, respect for a teacher is an artificial lie."

Much of what Neill describes as approved practice in his school sounds to the outsider very much like the license which he takes his stand against. Thus the boy who reported that he had broken some windows was encouraged by Neill to think that if he could pay for them, he might continue and break some more. Out in the real world we are not always permitted to indulge in destruction on the grounds that we can pay for that destruction afterward.

Many of Neill's notions seem to totally contradict the fairly well accepted principle of child training that through discipline imposed at first by others, the child gradually reaches the desirable goal of self-discipline.

Among the many freedoms which Neill considers essential for the child are: freedom from lessons or from being educated; freedom from moral teaching or training; freedom from sexual restraint; freedom from the inhibition of aggressive or destructive impulses. I shall discuss each of these in turn later on, but first a brief comment about Neill and Freud.

Neill's natural rebelliousness against authority is bolstered theoretically by two views: 1) his interpretation of Freudian doctrine; and 2) a rather conspicuous lack of knowledge about the way child behavior actually develops.

One of Neill's outstanding mistakes, a mistake so major that it invalidates his entire system, is his strong dependence on the Freudian notion that when a child is in difficulty, that is nearly always the fault of the parents. Neill believes that a child left to his own devices, and given complete freedom to express his natural impulses, will not be in trouble. This notion pervaded much of American thinking for many years. Fortunately, this idea is now no longer accepted in most circles. Yet Neill sticks with it. He starts out with the notion "There are no problem children, but only problem parents". He goes on to state:

> "I believe that a difficult child is nearly always made difficult by wrong treatment at home ... In the first five weeks or first five months (psychic) damage can be done to the child that lasts a lifetime."

He asks, "What makes a child neurotic?" And he answers: "In many cases it is the fact that his parents do not love each other." In sexual matters, especially, Neill claims that parents do serious harm to their offspring: "I have never had a pupil who did not bring to Summerhill a diseased attitude toward sexual and bodily functions." He implies that fortunately he got to them and straightened out most of these kids in time. This is a pretty pompous attitude. All the parents are wrong and only A. S. Neill is right.

This virtual hatred of parents is even stronger in Mr. Neill's second book *Freedom—Not License*. Thus, he advises a mother who is worried about her 17-year-old daughter's smoking: "Obviously, lady, you are out of touch with Janet and have been from her cradle days." How does he know?

There is little rebellion when there is nothing to rebel against. For heaven's sake, stop preaching to her now. Cigarettes will do her far less harm than her conviction that her mother is someone who is always lecturing her and forbidding something or other. Leave her be."

So much for parents. They are all pretty dreadful in Neill's opinion. According to him, grandparents are even worse. This distrust of parents and disgust with grandparents, as representing the adult world, is perhaps the reason that Neill refuses to identify with grown-ups. He appears rather to consider himself at one with his children. He does not want them to respect him, nor to revere him, nor to obey him, nor to look up to him. He not only does not require, but does not wish, that they should do anything for the sake of pleasing him. "To me, respect for a teacher is an artificial lie."

Neill's apparent disdain for all adults and his insistence on being merely another individual (another child?) suggests that not all adults are bad, wicked, and dangerous to their children's welfare, but merely that Neill has refused to grow up.

Neill states frankly:

"Summerhill is an island because (if it were part of a community) out of 100 parents, what percentage would approve of free choice in attending lessons?

Lessons at Summerhill are definitely optional. He emphasizes this again and again. Not only are lessons optional but books have little value for Neill. He emphasizes that "Books are the least important apparatus in school."

He reports with apparent pride that one of his students, a girl from a convent, loafed for three years. A boy named Tom came to Summerhill at the age of five and left at seventeen without having gone to a single lesson. (Possibly a record, even for Summerhill.) Mervyn was at Summerhill ten years and when he left at seventeen, he did not know how to read. (Later he taught himself.) Still others who had not learned much of anything in Summerhill classrooms later wanted to go to college and so they prepared themselves.

One can't help wondering what Tom and Mervyn and the others did while they were not attending classes or learning to read, other than expressing themselves, and developing their untrammelled personalities.

At any rate, the English School Inspector's report reads:

> *"On the whole the results of this system are unimpressive . . . The quality of the teaching, also, is unimpressive . . . The children lacked guidance. Summerhill is a difficult place in which to study."*

This last comment seems a rather telling criticism of that institution of learning, whatever its expressed philosophy.

Where Neill and I disagree starkly is that to me school is meant to be a place in which a child learns. For Neill, school is a place concerned with living and being happy. Even if one grants that the sole aim of education is to achieve happiness, I am not sure that happiness can in fact be achieved through Neill's hedonistic approach.

Neill argues for a child's freedom from any sort of moral teaching. He prefaces this notion by a statement proclaiming that children are "basically good". In one of his many inconsistencies, he later contradicts his first statement by saying that "When a mother teaches a child to be good, she suppresses the child's natural instincts." He stresses his belief that "There is no instance of cruelty nor any natural tendency toward malevolence in the child." A sweet thought but scarcely correct.

Neill believes that moral teaching is totally unnecessary because of a child's innate goodness: He says, "If your child lies, he is either afraid of you, or he is copying you." He emphasizes strongly that parents need not spend time teaching their child the difference between right and wrong, because "The child is never in the wrong." In fact, he goes so far as to state, "It is moral instruction that *makes* the child bad."

This, of course, is arrant nonsense. Anyone who has observed even a small number of children growing up appreciates the fact that very young children are quite prone to lie, steal, and otherwise misbehave. It takes much time, teaching, and experience before the ordinary child matures to a point where he can tell the truth, refrain from stealing, and otherwise conduct himself in a way that our society approves.

Neill's attitude that growing children should be given almost complete sexual freedom is one of the points for which he finds the fewest followers. Though there are indeed people who take this position, there are many others, not necessarily prudish people, who believe that even college students are more comfortable if a certain amount of restriction is imposed on them or at least suggested by the powers that be.

Not so Neill. With him, anything goes:

> *"In most schools there is a definite plan to separate boys from girls. Love affairs are not encouraged. They are not encouraged at Summerhill, either, but neither are they discouraged."*

He reports, with apparent pride, that when his daughter was

six years old, she told him. "Willie has the biggest cock among the small kids."

Though he insists that "Heterosexual play in childhood is the royal road to a healthy, balanced sexual life", and that "Adolescent sex life . . . is the right way to tomorrow's health", he does not go the whole way toward forming a society in which adolescents would be free to practice their own natural love lives because if he did, he says, he would be ruined, if not imprisoned as an immoral seducer of youth. And in a rather alarming non sequitur he asks parents, "Will the virginity of your daughter matter when the atomic bombs begin to drop?"

However he does permit what he considers a reasonable amount of sexual activity; but he points out to one young couple, "If you have a kid, it will ruin the school." In spite of this, he does not provide contraceptives for fear that the authorities might close the school.

As so often, he exaggerates the position of those he opposes and then criticizes the straw man he has built. Thus he insists that society's attitude toward birth—(and apparently toward sex in general)—is that it is "a dirty business, a shameful business." Not necessarily so, Mr. Neill.

Not only should children apparently be given complete sexual freedom, but more than that, they should be given complete freedom to express their aggressive, destructive impulses. Property is not important, but the child's need to express aggression and destructiveness *is*. If the child is inhibited in any way, there will be dire consequences, claims Neill. Thus he starts out with the basic premise:

> *"Children should not be compelled to respect property, for it always means some sacrifice of childhood's play life."*

He continues:

> *"Summerhill children do not go on to be criminals and mobsters after they leave school, because they are allowed to live out their gangsterdom (here) without fear of punishment and moral lectures."*

Neill points out that delinquency should be treated with understanding since *"behind every crime is a wish that had originally been a good one."* He holds that in order to rid a child of a bad social trait, one should let him live out his aggressive or destructive desires.

Thus he rewards stealing, and he encourages aggressive actions. And he boasts that if a child who was new to the school threw mud at a door he was painting, he would join him in the mud slinging "because his salvation is more important than the door."

Neill's defense of a youngster's destruction of property gives one the impression that he hates property as much as he hates parents. At any rate, his defense of the "normal, happy girl (who was) burning holes with a red-hot poker in a walnut mantlepiece" seems ridiculous. She explained that she "did it without thinking;" hence, since she did not do it "deliberately," there was really nothing wrong in her action, says Neill.

At any rate, the English School Inspectors who reported on Summerhill, did note that:

> *"Damages are heavier in Summerhill than in a disciplined school. Summerhill children are allowed to go through their 'gangster' period and consequently more furniture is destroyed."*

Neill's rejection of the importance of property and his insistence on the child's need to destroy, apparently goes far beyond that felt by his students. Thus he himself felt guilty when after the total destruction of his tools by the children, he locked up his new set. The children considered this move to be quite proper, but Neill felt that it was the wrong thing to do.

He states specifically:

> "The locking of doors has increased recently at Summerhill . . . Everybody voted to have the doors locked. I don't like it."

This is a very telling statement. It suggests the heart of my criticism. Neill constructs a theory of how a child thinks, and what he thinks the child needs, and even when that theory is refuted by all the objective evidence, he still insists on treating children *as if they were* as he imagined them to be.

Certainly it is not too difficult to be popular with children—apparently one of Neill's over-riding ambitions—if you let them do anything they want to, encourage them to be happy, and do not make any excessive attempts to teach them *anything*—either moral values, or respect for people or property, or academic facts.

That most of his students after going through a "gangster" period which lasts varyingly from months to years eventually settle down and stop breaking things is probably more due to the fact that even complete freedom becomes boring after a while, rather than to the correctness of Neill's concept.

I maintain that though children are not necessarily as naturally good as he thinks they are, neither are they the wild little beasts he describes, happy only if adults impose no restraint. Summerhill suggests that Neill is surprisingly ignorant about the way behavior develops and children grow and ignorant of what child specialists, in general, believe about the kind of handling that works best with young children, though he probably doesn't care about *that*.

Let's start with the self-demand type feeding of the infant which he seems to use as a prototype for all that comes after. He describes what he incorrectly calls self-*regulation*—he actually means self-*demand* here—as meaning "the right of a baby to live freely without outside authority in things psychic and somatic." He entirely omits, even right here at the beginning of the child's life, the second factor in self-demand, which was set up by Dr. Frances L. Ilg who first proposed this type of feeding regime at Yale University back in the 1930's.

The infant *is* fed when he makes the demand, but he is very quickly helped toward self-regulation. As the days go by, he is not fed *every single time* he cries. Contrary to Neill, there is an imposition of outside authority, or at least outside help. The baby gradually learns, with considerable help from his mother, to regulate his demand, until very quickly he has worked out for himself a reasonable schedule, satisfactory both to him *and* to his mother.

One second example of Neill's almost pathologic unwillingness to provide even the simplest, most harmless and most reasonable regulation, combined with a lack of knowledge of how children grow, is the episode of his little daughter's reaching for his glasses. His daughter Zoe, was just a year in age: "(she) showed a great interest in my glasses, snatching them off my nose to see what they were like. I made no protest, showed no annoyance. She soon lost interest in my glasses and never touched them. No doubt if I had sternly told her not to, her interest in my glasses would have survived, mingled with fear of me and rebellion against me."

This is a beautiful example of the kind of thinking which apparently led Neill into a permissiveness which seems not only unnecessary but a little ludicrous. Zoe was a little late in coming to her interest in glasses; but whether Neill had permitted the snatching or not, it is an interest that does not survive long in the normal infant, whether repressed or permitted. There are absolutely no data which prove that children who are inhibited from snatching glasses develop either fear or rebellion against the parent or person who, quite naturally, refuses to have his glasses snatched. Yet a whole theory of education has been built up by Mr. Neill based on such faulty thinking.

A third major error which Neill makes is that though he pays lip service to the fact that children differ from each other, his basic assumption is that all children dislike, and rebel against, and are harmed by discipline. He ignores the fact that many children are extremely conventional little creatures, who at least, at certain times, like to conform with the rules, and like to please the adult. This is a pleasure he insists on denying them. There are many children who like to "do it the right way;" many who are most comfortable with guidelines. Many others—wilder and less conforming—nevertheless do, at times, at least feel safer and more secure when they can find an adult who cares enough about them to make them conform.

Further minor errors or at least notions which go against much that we believe include the following: (I shall not try to prove that all these ideas are wrong. I shall merely offer my belief that these notions are incorrect.)

1. *Neill believes that though reward is not as bad as punishment, neither should be used with children.* Though I don't go as far as the *Operant Conditioning* people, I believe that both reward and punishment are useful and, if reasonably employed, harmless.

2. *Children should not do things to please other people.* I believe one of the young child's greatest pleasures is pleasing others. Why deprive him of it?

3. *Children should not respect authority, in fact, should not respect adults. Children should not be disciplined.* I believe the discipline of children is the first necessary step toward an adulthood in which they will, hopefully, achieve self-discipline. Respect for others is an essential step on the way to self-respect.

4. *Sex should be free, available and practiced as soon as the child matures sexually, if not before.* I believe that anyone who has observed the natural reticence not only of some young girls but even of boys, as they mature, may appreciate the fact that physical maturity is not all that is needed for readiness to perform sexually.

5. *Work is not necessary, play is paramount.* Neill obviously has not had the privilege of observing American children many of whom glory in the notion that they are *working*. In one of our normative groups, by far the majority, from second grade on, when asked what they liked to do best, replied "work", or named some special kind of schoolwork.

6. *The child cannot see cause and effect.* It appears that much of our research at the Gesell Institute and certainly much of Piaget's would contradict this notion.

7. *Children should be allowed to act out all their destructive impulses.* It seems to me that even some of our most permissive schools and clinics acknowledge that there comes a time when some restraint must be introduced if the destructive, aggressive or unhappy child is to progress toward more comfortable living.

In short, I deem Neill's whole approach to the development of a moral or ethical sense in the young child as quite incorrect.

Still another error, trivial—but I can't help mentioning it—is Neill's notion that if you give children total freedom they grow bigger, not only emotionally, but physically. Thus, he notes that "many of our boys at Summerhill grow to be six footers, even when their parents are comparatively short." I must point out that many children anywhere grow to be taller than their parents, but I surely doubt that it's the educational theory applied to them which results in their increased height.

Some of this criticism may be unduly harsh when one considers the kind of child who may for the most part, have turned up at Summerhill. In the early days of the school, according to Mr. Neill, the school was attended almost entirely by problem children. However, as time went on, the intake came to represent a fairly normal cross section of the population.

Certainly most of us admit that when one is dealing with very unusual children, very unusual methods must be used. The Green Valley School in Orange City, Florida, is a good example of a school run most successfully, more or less, along Summerhill lines. If I were a British clinician and Summerhill were available, it is quite likely that I would recommend this school or one like it to parents of a child who just does not fit in anywhere else.

But the kind of school needed for a child with a very special problem is often not desirable for those many quiet, academically inclined, conventional children who are most comfortable in a conventional school. Such children do not need the lack of regimentation and discipline offered by Summerhill; more likely they would be most disturbed by the lack of guidance, the poor opportunity for academic endeavor, the large number of classmates who might be setting fires or breaking windows or writing on the lavatory walls or just plain loafing for years and years.

Like many special types of education—Montessori, for instance, though in a quite different way—Neill's method might be expected to work well enough with those children who do not particularly need them, less well with some of those who perhaps do. Thus the bright, naturally academic and highly motivated child will, as a rule, even in a highly permissive school atmosphere, eventually come to terms with the idea of studying and learning something. However, such a child is often academically motivated enough to learn reasonably well and comfortably in the traditional school setting without his basic personality being disturbed by the structure. Such a child really doesn't need Summerhill.

On the other hand, the dull or less academically oriented child, when left to his own devices, doesn't ever necessarily come to terms with the idea of learning. Structure may be what he needs more, not less of, if he is to have any academic success whatever.

I would not choose to send the more ordinary or usual child to Summerhill for the following reasons:

1. I don't believe that the ordinarily constituted child needs this much freedom. I believe that many children enjoy and benefit by rather definite limits, rules, and regulations. This is true both in an academic setting and also true as far as the child's personal life is concerned. We once examined a rather disturbed boy who, for a while, had attended an extremely permissive school. The director of that school never lost his cool. We were told that finally the boy exploded and asked one of the instructors: "What do I have to do to get that guy mad at me?"

2. I see no value in everyone being brought down to the same level. All our years of work with children at Gesell suggest that whereas companionship and friendship between the old and the young is naturally desirable, most children, especially young children—are more comfortable and secure when the adults are willing to accept their adult role. It's easy and possibly gratifying to temporarily pretend that we are all at the same level. It's an easy way to make friends. But I think we owe children something more.

3. I agree with Vance Packard that in matters of sexual expression, young people must know what the adult standards are. They can rebel against them if they wish, or fail to meet them, but we owe it to them to at least give them a few restrictive guidelines.

4. I do not agree with Neill that the aim of life is happiness. I would not be comfortable to have a child for whom I was responsible exposed to, or saturated with, Mr. Neill's philosophy of life.

5. I do not share Neill's apparent contempt of books and of formal learning. I by no means agree that the purpose of attending school is *not* to learn.

Any professional person who is fully comfortable with what he is doing inevitably clings to his basic principles, but in my experience, he tends to mellow slightly as he ages; and often, as time goes, he can even grant a few points to those who hold other approaches or views. Not so with A. S. Neill. At least not to judge from his sequel to *Summerhill* which is entitled *Freedom—Not License.* In his follow-up volume, he appears to have become increasingly irritable, increasingly irascible, increasingly hostile to any who hold opposite views, increasingly unrealistic.

He takes to task all parents (including his own), all grandparents ("Keep your child as far away from his grandparents as possible"), clergymen, those who believe in Santa Claus, most everyone who lives in America.

He assures us that "Most men hate their work". He says "You should tell your child *exactly* what you think about his school." He says: "If your child refuses to do her homework, she is showing a healthy criticism of the system by refusing to take part in it." He claims, "If your home is a happy one, your son won't be likely to seek any form of religion." He declaims: "Spanking is symbolic of castration. It breaks the will, induces hate, can ruin a life." And goes on to pronounce the following:

> "If your child steals, you should pay him for his enterprise."

> "Parents must face the hard truth that they cannot do a thing about their adolescent children."

> "Every second American I meet seems to be in therapy."

Yet, at times, Neill comes through as a kinder man than his direct pronouncements indicate. He explains very simply that he started a school in order for there to be a place for children where emotions come first. He wanted to put emotions first because in his opinion, "nothing of importance comes from the head." He states quite frankly that the basic idea of Summerhill is that freedom must be tried, and that freedom never really *has* been tried.

Despite my logical disagreements, and in view of this softer approach, and judging from some of the pictures I've seen of Summerhill and of Neill with his young charges, my emotions, at times, are caught up in the feeling that just *maybe* there is something to all he has to say.

Born in New York in 1923, John Holt started teaching in grade schools at the age of thirty. During the next fourteen years he acquired a thorough firsthand knowledge of how elementary schools operate. He made his opinions on this subject known in two bestselling books, HOW CHILDREN FAIL *and* HOW CHILDREN LEARN. *He has also written articles for many journals of opinion, such as* HARPER'S, NEW YORK REVIEW OF BOOKS, PARENTS' MAGAZINE, *and* THE NEW YORK TIMES MAGAZINE. *His most recent book is entitled* THE UNDERACHIEVING SCHOOL.*

He has been a lecturer at the Harvard Graduate School of Education. At present, Mr. Holt serves as visiting lecturer in the Department of Education at the University of California in Berkeley.

John Holt

How does Summerhill work? What does it do, and how? What is the secret of Neill's art?

For answer, most people fall back on the word *love*. It won't do. Even if it were not widely misunderstood, abused, and exploited, even if we all agreed, as we do not, on what we meant by it, "love" is too simple and vague to be a good or complete explanation. It is no use to tell people that their child's problems will be solved if they will only love him. They think they do already. If they don't, they don't want to admit it, even to themselves.

Moreover, you can't make yourself love someone, feel affection, tenderness, joy in his company, by telling yourself that you ought to. Love in that sense is not to be turned on and off like a faucet. The problem is: what can be learned from Neill that can be applied by anyone, whatever he may feel or think he feels about children?

Over the years, many children have gone to Summerhill who were wholly defeated and demoralized by life, locked in their desperate protective strategies of self-defense and deliberate failure, filled with fear, suspicion, anger, and hatred. I knew one such child myself. Only a year before he went to Summerhill, he seemed not far from a complete breakdown. At Summerhill he got well. Most of the children there—not all, the school has had its failures—get well. They get back their strength, confidence, and courage, and turn to face life and to move out into it, as all healthy children really want to do, instead of running and hiding from it. In a school that does not care much about schoolwork many of these children, hopeless failures in school after school, begin to do competent and even excellent work, often progressing two, three, and even five times as fast as conventionally good students in conventionally good schools.

How does Neill help such children get well and start living again? Many people will start arguing here about what they call "Permissiveness." The argument is silly and useless. So is the word itself. Like so many pejorative words—"growl words" as a friend of mine calls them—"permissiveness" sticks a two-valued label on a complicated, multi-valued, even multi-dimensioned reality. Black *or* white. Permissive *or* not permissive. Permissive of what? Nobody in the world—not even the most fanatic kind of old-fashioned, complex-fearing progressivist—permits a child to do *everything*. And nobody, except those few twisted souls who like to chain a child to a bedpost or lock him in a closet, permits a child to do nothing. Some permit some things, others permit others. What A permits, B forbids.

Thus, for example, I like to talk to little children, and to listen to them talk. I take their talk and ideas seriously. I do not think that their view of life or their opinions on it are trivial because they are based on little experience. I like to do what many sneeringly call "getting down to their level"—play games with them, foolish games, rough games, even games where they hit me or call me names, provided only that the spirit is joyous and friendly. I do not demand of them the kind of enlisted-man-to-officer deference that most adults think is their right. But I will not buy children candy and junk every time we happen to go in a store, and I make this clear to them before we go in. We must take children seriously and treat them courteously and respectfully, but we should not, as most people do, constantly indulge them with money.

Dealing with children, some people draw lines here, others there. All of us draw them differently for different children and different circumstances. The word "permissiveness" cannot possibly describe all the variations and subtleties of these lines. More to the point, it cannot describe the spirit in which these lines are drawn. There are many ways of telling a child that he must go to bed at a certain hour. A may sincerely believe that if the child is not told when to go to bed, his sleep and his health will suffer, and that he will develop bad habits. B may sincerely believe that a child expects, needs, and demands to be told when to go to bed. C may simply sweep a child off to bed at a certain hour because he wants to get him out of the way. D may tell him to go to bed, as he tells him many other things, because he thinks it is good for the child to be made to do what he doesn't want to do. E may tell him to go to bed because he needs to push someone around and his child happens to be the handiest and perhaps the only person he *can* push around. One parent may say, "This hurts me more than it does you," and mean it; another may say, "This hurts you more than it does me," and enjoy it. These differences make all the difference.

Conversely, one may *not* tell a child to go to bed for many widely different reasons. A may sincerely believe that if going to bed is not made a field of battle a child will sensibly regulate his own sleep, decide when to go to sleep as he decides when to run or get a drink or sit down. B may want a child to learn by experience the consequences of not getting enough sleep, so that eventually, even if not right away, he will be able to manage this part of his life. C may believe that it is bad to *make* a child go to bed, or do anything else, that he doesn't want to do. D just may not care. E may shrink from a painful battle he is not sure he can win, or that seems more trouble than it is worth. F, fearing he may lose the love of his child, may give him his way as a kind of bribe. Again, these differences make all the difference, and the difference they make varies much from one child to another. Some children are very sensitive to punishment; others not at all. Some children are little affected by attempts to bribe them, some are insulted and angered, some—the only ones properly called "spoiled"—are deeply corrupted.

In any case, to call Neill permissive is not just an oversimplification but a serious mistake. Let me cite an example that is widely, indeed almost always misunderstood—the matter of his rewarding with a gift a child who steals something. When Neill gives a child sixpence for stealing, is he "permitting" him to steal? Nonsense! If Neill meant to "permit" it, didn't care whether a child stole or not, he would simply take no notice. But in fact he takes a very particular kind of notice, whose meaning is not for a second lost on the child. The child knows, when Neill gives him the sixpence, that he is not saying, "Sure, stealing is fine, go steal some more." The child knows already that Neill does not steal and does not want stealing around the school. What then does he hear Neill saying with this gift of sixpence? He hears him saying, "I know you are not a thief." He is rightly amazed, thinks, "Not a thief! Of course I'm a thief, everyone tells me so, all the time. Besides, I just proved it, by stealing." To these thoughts he hears Neill's silent reply, "No, not a thief. If I thought you were a thief, and would go on stealing indefinitely, I'd be a bloody idiot to give you money every time you did it, wouldn't I?" No way to argue with that; Neill is clearly no idiot. "No, at heart you're not a thief. You may be stealing *now*, trying to satisfy important needs that you don't know how to satisfy any other way. But there are other ways. I am ready to help you look for them, and I think you will find them."

Among the Father Brown detective stories by G. K. Chesterton—wonderful stories, by the way—there is a particularly moving story called *The Secret of Flambeau*. In the story a great American detective is discussing crime and criminals with Father Brown and his old friend Flambeau, the long retired and now respectable one-time master criminal and terror of Europe. The American has asked

Father Brown the secret of his success at catching criminals. Father Brown answers that it is simple, he has only to put himself into the mind, the very heart and soul of the criminal, see and feel things as he does, *become* the criminal himself, to know who the criminal is. The American can't take this, cannot admit that there is a potential criminal in everyone, in himself, angrily dismisses all this as sentimentality. This is too much for Flambeau. He rises to his full, enormous height, tells the American who he is, that the police of the entire world tried without success for years to catch him, that only Father Brown had understood why he stole, and that when he told him why he stole he had stopped stealing for good. A romantic story, perhaps, but there seems to me a truth in it that Neill has understood.

Like Father Brown, Neill understands the importance of forgiveness and faith, notions that many contemporary thinkers consider old-fashioned and unmeasurable, hence unscientific. Perhaps the recent work of Robert Rosenthal[1] may convince at least some that the behavior we expect of people has a great deal to do with the behavior we are likely to get.

Neill also understands something about Operant Conditioning that is overlooked or not understood by many of its practitioners and worshippers. What they call Positive Re-enforcement, and what plain English calls encouragement or reward, depends not on the view of the person who gives it but the person who gets it. Human motives are a good deal more complicated than those of rats or pigeons. From outside another person's mind and skin we can only guess, we cannot know what *he* may sense as re-enforcement. Thus a child who for years has stolen repeatedly is quite obviously getting something he thinks he wants, i.e., being re-enforced, by whatever the adults are doing and saying to try to make him stop.

[1] *Pygmalion In The Classroom*, Holt, Rinehart, & Winston

Finally Neill knows something almost too simple and everyday to be called psychology, which is that if telling a child for years not to steal and punishing him when he does has not made him stop, it is time to try something else.

What is the something else? The sixpences—and not every wrong act is rewarded—are only a part of it. More important is Neill's way of reacting to offenses and offenders, perhaps better called the natural collisions of wills, interests, and needs in his small close-knit community. He may not always reward, or even approve. He may even get indignant or angry. But whatever he does, he is responding to the act itself, not sitting in judgement on a person. What he tries to deal with is the fact that Tommy has just stolen something, not that Tommy "is a thief." Also, his response is of the moment, not permanent. He does not label children, does not make a permanent record of their past offenses, does not pile black marks and demerits on them. The children do not feel that mistakes are indefinitely held against them, don't have to drag their unhappy pasts behind them, feel they have a fresh start each day—and which of us does not need and want that.

Also, his response is personal. Though now and then, as head of the school, he may have to decide that a particular child, being more disturbed or destructive than the school can handle, cannot stay there, most of the time he reacts not as "authority", not as some embodiment of right and virtue, but as Neill. If, as occasionally he must, he speaks sternly or even angrily, he is speaking for himself, not all of humanity. Thus he does not make the child feel that he has been cast out of humanity. In this, how much wiser he is than most of our judges, who often preach little moral lessons at the men they are sending off to prison; probably nothing guarantees so much as those lessons the quickest possible return of those men to crime.

Because Neill's reaction is immediate, personal, and authentic, not impersonal, bureaucratic, and assumed, it is instructive. Now and then, as when a child swipes one of his garden tools just when he needs to use it, he may get angry. His anger conveys to children what really is wrong about stealing—that it hurts the person you steal from. It has nothing to do with anything so abstract and foolish, not to say mistaken, as the notion that property and property rights are sacred. What counts is that when you take something from someone you inflict on him a time and energy wasting, anxious, painful experience. He hunts frantically for the missing object, can't find it, tries to think where he might have put it, wonders whether he might have left or lost it somewhere else, wonders whether someone else might have borrowed it and forgot to tell him, wonders later whether whoever took it will remember to return it, or even means to return it, wonders, if it was taken on purpose, which of his enemies or even friends might have done it, wonders perhaps whether his friends really are his friends. All this hurts. Moreover, whatever it was he wanted to do, he can't do, because of what is missing. When we steal from people, this is what we do to them. They hate it, and we shouldn't do it. This is what children learn from the quick and natural anger of people from whom they steal.

Enough has been said about the general meetings at Summerhill (most non-coercive schools have similar meetings) so that I need only note here that they serve, not only as the body that makes most of the laws of the school, but also as a kind of court where disputes may be settled and offenses by one person against another dealt with. At the meeting I attended, a small boy "brought up", as the school saying goes, a bigger boy for bullying him. He told his story, the bigger boy told his, witnesses spoke up, the small boy's story was established as true, and the bigger boy shamefacedly admitted it. What to do? The chairman asked the big boy angrily—this had come up before—why he didn't leave the little boy alone. The big boy muttered something about not being able to stand him. Several children said, "Then stay away from him; he doesn't follow you around." Another child pointed out that they had to do more than this to make it less likely that the bullying would happen again. Soon the children hit on a most practical and human solution. They realized with the wisdom of children that punishing the big boy would probably do more harm than good. Instead, they agreed that if the little boy was bullied again, he should have the right to call an instant school meeting, taking precedence over anything else that might be going on. Thus the bigger boy would face, immediately, the community's disapproval of his bullying, plus their additional annoyance at having been diverted by this matter from whatever they had been doing. I don't know how this all came out, but it seems a much wiser way of dealing with the problem than any group of adults would be likely to devise.

One might ask, why any bullying at all in such a community—and from other sources I have heard that at one time or another bullying has been a problem at the school. The reason is simple enough. Unhappy kids, like unhappy adults, are apt to try to work off their frustration and anger on whatever scapegoats they can find. Also, until very recently and perhaps even now, the ritualized bullying of little kids by big ones was allowed and even encouraged in many British schools. One might also ask, might not the school meeting itself sanction the harassing of an unpopular student, as in the horrifying story in Frank Conroy's autobiography *Stop-Time*, in which he and the other students at a so-called progressive American school decide by unanimous vote that all of them, each in turn, would punch in the jaw as hard as they could a boy they all disliked. The answer is that if such a thing had ever been proposed at Summerhill, which I doubt, Neill and the other adults would never have allowed it.

In any free community, majority rights are not absolute. They must always be limited by some overriding sense of what is fair and just. In any free school worthy of the name, the adults provide this limitation of the right of the majority to do what it pleases.

What else in the school helps children to get well? Children there do many things that most adults, in home or at school, will not let them do—swear, be dirty, wear raggedy clothes, break things. At the meeting I went to, a girl of about twelve contentedly sucked her thumb throughout the meeting, taking it out now and then to make some astute comment. Nobody teased her or seemed to take any notice. Is there something intrinsically therapeutic about being able to use four letter words, or go for days without a bath? I doubt it. What seems more important is that these children were freed from the enormous pressure under which they had been living. For many of them, life before Summerhill must have seemed one long battle, most of it against adults whose love or good will they needed and wanted. A hundred times a day they must have had to face the agonizing decision: shall I do what Mother, or Father, or Teacher, or Authority, tells me, or not? What do I stand to gain? What to lose? These are not light calculations. Having to make them day after day must be exhausting to children, as it would be to any of us. They had to spend so much time and energy either doing or not-doing what others told them to do that they had no time and energy for doing things on their own. One way or another they were always reacting to others, giving in or resisting, but in neither case were they acting independently, autonomously, or pursuing their own interests and needs.

At Summerhill they are free of this. They do not have to decide all the time what to do about the people who are trying to force them to do things, because nobody is forcing them. As long as they don't interfere with other children's lives, they can do what they want, or as little as they want. At last, they have time. Time even to "do nothing"—though in fact this is impossible, nobody alive can "do nothing," awake or asleep our minds are working, usually on things important to us. What then are the children doing who seem to be "doing nothing," and how does it help them? Here I can only guess, drawing on what I can remember of the ways I have used thoughts or dreams or fantasies to overcome or digest or somehow get the better of experiences that had at first got the better of me. I suspect that much of the time they are thinking over their lives, their past, playing it over and over, reliving it, reworking it, until they have robbed it of some of its power to cripple and hurt.

Years ago I heard the psychoanalyst Theodore Reik give to young lovers, married or otherwise, what seemed a most astonishing piece of advice. *Don't,* he said, get into the business of talking over your happy memories of meeting, courtship, love, etc. Don't sit around saying fondly, "Remember that time we . . ." As long as that memory lives in your subconscious, the experience will keep its magic power and will nourish your love for each other. But if you drag it up into the bright daylight of consciousness and talk, it will begin to fade like an old photograph in the sun, lose its freshness and intensity, become like something seen or read or that happened to someone else. It seemed to follow from this— whether he said it or not I no longer remember—that the way to rob a past experience of its power to hurt is not to try to forget it, but to try to remember it, over and over again.

Do this, and an odd thing happens. At first, remembering the experience, you literally relive it, are right in the middle of it. Then, gradually, you begin to draw away from it, get outside it. Whatever happened to you, you still see and hear, but increasingly as a spectator, as if watching a movie of yourself. At first the movie is vivid and painful, all close-ups, and that really is you in the middle of it. But as you play that movie over and over, it becomes less vivid and real, and that person there in the midst of it, having bad things happen to him or making some kind of dreadful fool of himself, is not the here-and-now living you, but a part you once played, a you that no longer exists.

And as you draw out of and away from that experience, you may begin to do something else, have that character in there play his role differently, avoid his mistake, say or do something other and better than what he did. You begin to reshape the past. We all do this. I think of an example, trivial but typical. Last winter, starting on a fairly complicated series of air trips, I put my ticket into my pocket. When near the airport, too far to turn back, I realized that my tickets were in two envelopes, and that I had left behind the more important of them. I raged at myself for a while, and then, in my fantasy world, I began to replay the scene in my room as I should have played it. I saw myself carefully looking in the file folder where the other ticket was, taking it out, putting it in my pocket. I saw myself doing a number of things that, had I really done them, would have reminded me to look for that second book of tickets. After a while I was no longer angry at myself, no longer distressed by the experience, able to see it as just another goof-up, ready to go on to whatever life brought next.

What is the use of these mental tricks? I have suggested one: by replaying the experience we get away from it and outside it. Also, by adjusting the past we create as it were a new past or pasts, in which we were more sensible, prudent, closer to the kind of person we want to be. These made-up pasts can be a kind of preparation for the future. They are a way, perhaps the only way, to learn from our mistakes. Not only do we prepare ourselves to act better in the future, but to some extent we fool ourselves that we really did act a little better in the past. We see our real selves, the selves most real to us, not as that person who goofed back there, but as the person who thought—even if too late—of the sensible thing to do. So, imagining myself *not* forgetting instead of forgetting that airline ticket, or, as on another occasion, *not* locking my keys in my car, I am able to get the dunce cap off my head.

It seems very likely that children do some such things. It seems likely, too, that the fantasies by means of which they rework and get control of the past may be much wilder than my own humdrum efforts. Little children in their free dramatic play take all kinds of mythic and animal roles; perhaps they do the same in the privacy of their minds. At any rate, whatever the mechanism may be, the experience of Summerhill and like places has proved that in the human mind and spirit are healing powers comparable to those in the body. If the wounds in our souls are not rubbed raw and torn open each day, many of them will heal. This is what Summerhill makes possible.

It also gives children a chance, and this may too be a part of the healing process, to manage a great deal of their lives, to make decisions and to find out from their living which are better or worse than others, and from so doing begin to feel that they *can* make decisions, that not all of these will *necessarily* be bad, that if they are bad they can see this and make changes, that they are smart and capable enough to make some sense of their lives, and don't need indefinitely to depend on the guidance or commands of others. In short, more by what it does than says, Summerhill helps the children there to feel, and often for the first time, that they are human beings of some dignity, competence, and worth. Children get well and grow at Summerhill because of the freedom, support, and respect it gives them, and these conditions of freedom, support, and respect are the minimum conditions we must establish in other schools if we want health and growth for the children there. No educational reforms that do not *begin* here seem to me worthy of much attention, or likely to make any real or lasting improvements in the lives and learning of our children.

The key word is *begin*. The worst thing that can happen to any great pioneer of human thought is for his ideas to fall into the hands of disciples and worshippers, who take the living, restless, ever-changing thought of their master and try to carve it into imperishable granite, so that not a word shall ever be lost or changed. The words may remain, but the spirit is soon lost. A friend of mine used to say, "A conservative is a man who worships a dead radical." Nowhere is this more true than in education; one thinks immediately of Maria Montessori and John Dewey. It would be a tragedy if it happens to Neill. The only way to prevent it, to honor Neill as he deserves, is to try to continue the exploration he started, to move on further into the uncharted territory of human freedom, happiness, and growth. We must therefore take Neill's thought, his writing, his work, and Summerhill itself, not as a final step, but as a first one.

Bruno Bettelheim holds two professorships at the University of Chicago: he is the Stella M. Rowley Distinguished Service Professor of Education and is also Professor of Psychology and Psychiatry. He is also Director of the Orthogenic School, the University's residential treatment center for severely emotionally disturbed children.

Born in Vienna, he received his Ph.D. in psychology and philosophy from the University of Vienna. He came to this country in 1939.

Some of his books, such as THE EMPTY FORTRESS, LOVE IS NOT ENOUGH, *and* TRUANTS FROM LIFE *describe the work of the Orthogenic School in rehabilitating severely disturbed youngsters. Others deal with problems of social psychology and related issues. His most recent book* CHILDREN OF THE DREAM *discusses communal childrearing in the Israeli kibbutzim and its implications for American education. Other works include:* SYMBOLIC WOUNDS, THE INFORMED HEART, SOCIAL CHANGE AND PREJUDICE, *and* DIALOGUES WITH MOTHERS.

Bruno Bettelheim

Re-reading Neill's work after some 30 years was quite an experience; the more so since I had imagined myself most familiar with his thinking all those years. I refer to his germinal book, *The Problem Child*, which appeared in 1926 and had a deep and immediate impact on all those concerned with psychoanalytically oriented education. But so much has happened in the last quarter-century, even in the ten years since his book *Summerhill* was published in this country; and so grossly have Neill and his work been misunderstood, that I can only strongly advise re-reading him as I did with today's educational problems in mind. I urge this especially for everyone concerned with the well-being of children, and for those specifically interested in what we do wrong in our methods of education.

Though Neill's work was familiar to me from the 20's, it was only after *Summerhill* appeared that I began to have frequent occasion to be annoyed with implications being drawn from his writings by his American readers. Occasionally, I was even carried away, blaming him in my own mind for how they misread him and misapplied his teaching, though I should have known better. But so persuasive were his enthusiastic followers, so insistent that their own exaggerations and distortions truly represented his educational philosophy, so convinced were they that they read him correctly, that even I was slowly swayed. Little by little I began to think of Neill as somewhat foolish in his all-permissive-ness—I, of all people, who should have known better. Because I, too, have been confronted with the same double problem: How, in general, does one apply a psychoanalytic understanding of man to the education of children in a residential setting; and how does

one apply psychoanalytic understanding to the needs of a particular group of children? In Neill's case, this meant a group of
relatively normal or only mildly disturbed children; in my own
case, the most severely disturbed children there are.

On still other grounds, I had run into similar misunderstand-
ings of my writings for over two decades. I had always blamed
myself for them, thinking I should have done better at explaining
myself. Which again made re-reading *Summerhill* a salutary experience. Because to think of the distortions evoked by Neill's
writing—from admirers no less than from critics—was to recognize
how little he and his writings were to blame. Personally, it was
a relief. Because I can now comfort myself that where my writings
were distorted and misunderstood, they are less to blame than
those preconceived notions which the reader finds support for,
no matter what the author has really said or has had in mind.

Now why was it particularly easy for Neill's work to be so
grossly distorted? I believe because Neill the person and the
educator is so much greater a man, so much more deeply human,
so much more outstanding a molder of youth, than he is a
philosopher or a student of psychoanalysis, or a theoretical psychologist. Though all his actions show how deeply attuned he is
to the psyche of children, he is often at a loss to explain himself.
That is why he is best in the many examples of how he operates,
and why his book is essentially a set of examples. But it is also
why, though his examples are rich in psychological wisdom, he is
often woefully inadequate and naive when he tries to explain. For
then, he is not even above dodging an issue with a sleight of hand
as when asked, for example, why he plays down the teaching of
Latin or mathematics, and he replies, "If the experts in mathematics and Latin have great minds, I have never been aware of
it." For Neill is quite aware that among mathematicians, as among
Latinists, great minds are as frequent—that is, as rare—as they are

among persons of any other calling. What Neill would know, better than anyone, is how to deal with a child who wants to concentrate on those subjects, or how to accept with deep empathy the child who wants nothing to do with those subjects. But when posed as a theoretical question, the great clinician of education is at a loss, and takes too simple a way out.

Or in a more serious vein: When asked how he justifies his prohibiting intercourse among his pre-adolescent students, he replies that his school would otherwise be closed. Which is probably true, but it hardly clarifies the deeper issue: If he believes—as I have no doubt he does—that no sexual activity should be inhibited, how does such sexual activity affect the psychology of a pre-pubertal girl, what does it do to her view of herself, later on, if she has intercourse, even if at the moment she was attracted to it? What would happen to a thirteen-year-old if she got pregnant? How would that affect her development, in our society, if she was either forced to give up her child, or compelled to become a mother long before she wanted to?

Having said this, I have no doubt that should one of his children become pregnant, he would help her to deal with her predicament with the utmost sensitivity and understanding. But in today's world, a terrible predicament it would nevertheless be. And since not all of us have a school to keep open, it hardly meets the problem of whether or not to bless pre-adolescent sexual intercourse in our society, nor does his philosophy suggest how to prevent such activity, if we do not approve of it.

That his girls do not get pregnant, that the very great freedom he accords them is so salutary for them, is because most of the children who come to him were raised in a Victorian atmosphere of severest repression. Many come from British public schools with their repressive practices; from homes where spanking brought obedience; and with sexual taboos rigorously imprinted.

Even after he has lifted innumerable prohibitions, these children are left with enough of a superego to prevent excess. More important, it makes the man who has freed them of so much crippling anxiety beloved to them, so that soon they cannot help but identify with him.

But this would never work with children who had too little superego to begin with, as is true for so many of our difficult children, whether raised in slums or in over-indulgent homes. What Neill fails to see is the extent to which his system works because it is the very antidote for the disease they suffer from— over-repression. That is why he can believe that what is good medicine for those who suffer crippling inhibitions is also the best for all—which it is not.

In his philosophizing, Neill is thus charmingly naive. One can and does love him for his naivety; it is so much part of what is so very good in him. But if one tries to apply his philosophy as he states it, rather than flexibly applying what the man really stands for, then one does indeed end up making a fool of the man and his teaching.

Neill's basic philosophy is naively Rousseauean, with the human infant born inherently good. If only evil society, especially his bad parents, were to let the child grow up naturally without anxieties and inhibitions, he would mature all on his own, into the most glorious human being. As for psychoanalysis, Neill has taken from it only that repression is bad, and that neuroses are brought on by sexual inhibitions.

True, Neill wrote before ego psychology became the corner-stone of psychoanalytic theory and practice. But he remains unaware that while anxiety causes neurosis, anxiety is also what keeps society going. Anxiety is also the mainspring of creativeness, of invention, and of progress, to borrow an old-fashioned nine-teenth century term. Yes, anxiety about loss of self-respect is even the well-spring of Neill's own success, which can only be described by another pair of old-fashioned virtues: personal honesty and common decency. He is utterly honest in all his human interactions, and his highest value is common decency, which he expects the children to make their own guiding principle.

But he fails to take account of the existential anxiety which, according to some psychoanalysts, originates in separation anxiety. Nor does he talk about our deep inner conflicts or our psycho-social crises: He takes no note of the continuous battle between id and superego, of eternal eros against the instinct of aggression, to mention only some of these conflicts. His naive optimism stands here in stark contrast to Freud's pessimism about human nature.

Neill's simple views of man, and why things go wrong with man, contradict those of Freud who recognized the inner complexities man is heir to, and which cause his eternal inner struggles. This is because Neill came to psychoanalysis by way of the Wilhelm Reich of the *Function of the Orgasm,* the Reich who held that the source of man's conflicts is society, and not the nature of man. Eventually, Reich's failure to integrate psychoanalysis and communism forced him into cosmic speculations, and to putting man in an orgone box. Neill's greater closeness to life and to children kept him from ever putting children into boxes.

But lacking psychological sophistication—sophisticates never understand children, who are so obvious if we can accept their obviousness—Neill remains unaware of why the things he does work. He believes they work because he's on the side of the children, which indeed he is. Since he believes they are born without sin, that their difficulties come not from within themselves but from a bad society, nothing more is needed than to protect them from society, to take their side against it. Would that things were that simple.

Since Neill does not worry about psychology, about how exactly the changes in his students come about, he does not face the fact that all is due to how they identify with him. He does not realize that Summerhill works not because it is just the right setting in which to raise children, but because it is nothing but an extension of his personality. Everything about it expresses Neill. From the moment they come to Summerhill, children are enveloped by Neill, by what he stands for and lives for. Everywhere there is the powerful impact of his person, most of all his common decency. And sooner or later, most children come to identify with him, however reluctantly. When, for example, a child calls him a fool, Neill believes this is a salutary effect of having given the child the freedom to oppose him. But the child does not oppose him; he loves him. Neill has indeed given him freedom—so much so, that trust was born; trust enough to couch a declaration of love and admiration in a somewhat abusive form.

Since the changes Neill produces in his children are based on identification, he succeeds only with those who can identify with him. And many can, because he is simply one of the grandest men around. But let a smaller person try to apply his naive philosophy, and chaos would follow. Because Neill's view of man is simply incorrect, though his view does inspire him to feats of true greatness. Most of all, Neill is all of a piece with hardly a flaw in his personality—excepting always his naiveté. In a great man, this is rather an asset. But what a liability it becomes in smaller men!

Having now been head of a boarding school for a quarter of a century, I cannot help comparing Neill's experiences with ours at the Orthogenic School of the University of Chicago. My re-evaluation of Neill's book will thus be flavored by my own convictions and experiences, and of these I must in fairness warn the reader. But with that caution, I might say that what far outweighs Neill's lack of psychoanalytic depth is his deep respect for the child as a unique human being. Implied in all that he says—though he is explicit enough when talking about parents—is that one cannot truly respect another person unless one respects oneself highly.

Among other things, one's self-respect requires that one does not make a fool of oneself. Certainly, respect for a child entails our not letting the child make a fool of himself. But this is exactly where so many followers of Neill go astray and completely misunderstand what he teaches. That is, they pervert his teaching of true freedom to imply that one should permit a child to make a fool of himself, the adult, or both, all equally destructive; in short, that one should give a child enough rope to hang himself. Essential to everything Neill says is that we must teach a child to understand what a rope is all about, so that he will never use it to hang himself or another.

When Neill wrote *The Problem Child* in 1926, it was directed to the readers and problems of his time. Since most children who came to him then were suffering from a too rigid, too punitive type of rearing, he was mostly concerned with showing the evils that led to. Nowadays, many children suffer far more from a reverse kind of rearing, namely of having things too much their way. Those who believe that this is what Neill recommends should read: "To let a child have his own way, or do what he wants to *at another's expense,* is bad for the child. It creates a spoiled child, and the spoiled child is a bad citizen."

How aware he is that we cannot permit immature minds to impose their will on us may be illustrated by the story of a boy who was trying to terrorize others. " 'Cut it out my boy,' I said sharply, 'we aren't afraid of you.' He dropped the hammer and rushed at me. He bit and kicked me. 'Every time you hit or bite me,' I said quietly, 'I'll hit you back.' And I did. Very soon he gave up the contest and rushed from the room."

Here is a lesson for some of our permissive parents and schools. What Neill knew even then, and what everyone not shackled by his preconceived notions soon learns, is that to submit to coercion leaves both child and adult with nothing but hatred or contempt for each other. If we permit someone to coerce or intimidate us, we stop being of much use to that person. We cannot help them because they do not respect us; and furthermore, we can not help them because we dislike them, whether or not we admit that to ourselves.

Every one of Neill's specific reactions—as opposed to his stated philosophy—remains valid even for situations he could not possibly have considered because those situations did not exist at the time *Summerhill* was published. Neill's criteria apply because they stem from his deep respect for the person. This may be illustrated by what he says on the very first page of *Freedom—not License*, his follow-up on *Summerhill*: "I define license as interfering with another's freedom. For example, in my school a child is free to go to lessons or stay away from lessons because that is his own affair, but he is not free to play a trumpet when others want to study or sleep." Maybe the passage hit me because student activists had just interrupted one of my classes believing, as do many of Neill's American followers, that they were fighting for their freedom, while in fact they were undermining all freedom by practicing license.

Would that our militant students, concerned as they are with their individual freedom, with being authentic and creating a better society, had learned what Neill, that great educator, considers the basic requirement for any better society: namely, respect for the individual. One must be convinced that one has no right to interrupt what others are doing, though one has every right to abstain from what is being done if that is his wish.[1]

From our own experience, I can only underscore what Neill says about the freedom of the child. "It all sounds easy and natural and fine, yet it is astounding how many parents, keen on the idea, manage to misunderstand it." And he cites the example of parents who let their four-year-old son bang on a neighbor's piano with a wooden mallet, looking on with a triumphant smile, meaning, "Isn't self-regulation wonderful?" This is what I meant earlier when I spoke of parents who give their child enough rope, not to hang himself by, but to make a fool of himself and of them. They are the same "young enthusiasts for self-regulation [who] come to my school as visitors, and exclaim at a lack of freedom in locking poison in a closet, or our prohibition about playing on the fire escape. The whole freedom movement is marred and despised because so many advocates of freedom have not got their feet on the ground . . . One such protested to me recently because I shouted sternly to a problem boy of seven who was kicking my office door."

[1] In defense of many militant students I should add that they respond to what might be called "Summerhill" methods of education, which are simply good educational methods, period. The group who tried to break up my class did so because they were annoyed with a statement I had made. Understandably so, given their views. Since in my classes I discuss only what the students want to talk about, I told them I was quite ready to do just that. I invited them to say what they had on their minds, which they did for a while. Then the rest of the class, on their own, voted by overwhelming majority that the group should desist, and that I should continue from where we left off. Before doing so, I encouraged those who preferred to hear further what the militants had to say to meet separately with them, because I did not believe they would profit from my teaching when they thought there was something else which was more important to listen to. With that the militants left. It was a large class, and I do not know how many left with them, but the majority did not. Since I really meant what I said, the militants left—angry with me, but in peace.

Because I respected them and their concerns, they were able, in return, to respect mine. But this, of course, does not work as a trick. Emotionally wrought up persons, more than others, "smell" if one really cares about their needs. They can respect the other person's needs, only if they feel that their needs have been respected first.

One more delightful story to show Neill's common sense—that characteristic most needed in all our dealings with children—and how sorely lacking it is in those who neither understand the value of freedom nor the viciousness of license: "A woman brought her girl of seven to see me. 'Mr. Neill,' she said, 'I have read every line that you have written; and even before Daphne was born, I decided to bring her up exactly along your lines.' I glanced at Daphne who was standing on my grand piano with her heavy shoes on. She made a leap for the sofa and nearly went through the springs. 'You see how natural she is,' said the mother. 'The Neillian child!' I fear that I blushed."

Having so often had the identical experience with parents who had read every line I have written without understanding my meaning at all, my heart went out to Neill. "It is this distinction between freedom and license that many parents never grasp." But then he goes on to explain that "The proper home is one in which children and adults have equal rights." And here, as in many other places, while in total agreement with Neill's meaning, I think it better to talk of appropriate rights than of equal rights. Because the right to play with guns means very little to adults, as the right to read in peace means very little to the young child. So it is an appropriate right for the child to play with guns, as it is the appropriate right of adults to read in peace.

Perhaps I am in a better position than most to judge what is involved in operating a Summerhill. For example, in my own work, as at Summerhill, boys and girls come to us as young as age five, and others as late as fifteen or older, and these children will remain with us for many years.

What most readers of *Summerhill* do not understand is that while such an educational setting imposes few specific demands, though never trivial ones, it is really among the most demanding of educational institutions. Because such a setting demands of the child that he develop a very high degree of self-respect; and with it, true respect for others. This is much harder to learn than how to automatically get to class at 9:00 o'clock, and to pay attention when there. It is even harder than Latin or trigonometry.

Applying this to the particular problems of the Orthogenic School, I am always impressed with how, on casual acquaintance with our institution, visitors are astonished by the so-called "un-demandingness" about etiquette, manners, and behavior. Because with us, the inner attitude toward children is much like Neill's, though with different children and a different philosophy, our practices are quite different. What visitors overlook is that the avoidance of minor demands has a purpose, and that that purpose is to free the child's energy for the enormous task of rebuilding his misdeveloped personality.

To concentrate on so major a task and to do it in ways that are both age-correct for the child and with respect for the child's freedom, means doing things that many peace-loving, middle-class parents in America cannot accept. It means that if children want to play with guns and act out battles, we must respect such desires. We must not be so distrustful of them as to assume that if they play war as children, they will therefore grow up to be war-loving, murderous adults.

By playing at war, these children can realize in their own ways what is wrong with war. If we do not push them into a particular mold concerning war and peace, they can later, as grownups, be free of the military spirit. Instead, the modern peace-loving parent forbids all war games. I, therefore, wish all parents could re-read what Neill says of children at Summerhill who when they want to make things, "always [make] a toy revolver or boat or kite." He understands how little difference there is to the child between a revolver or a gun, and a boat or a kite. The difference between them exists only in the mind of the adult, not in the mind of the child. And the adult who imposes this difference on the child destroys the child's freedom.

In another context Neill tells us that: "A parent's fear of the [child's] future affords a poor prognosis for the health of the child. This fear, oddly enough, shows itself in the desire that his children should learn more than he [the parent] has learned." It is the parent who has never really learned to control his own aggressive impulses who also feels the greatest need to keep his child from playing war games. But in this way, he convinces the child of how deeply he distrusts him as a person. Because the parent seems convinced that as the child grows older, he will not be able, on his own, to decide that peaceful cooperation is better than violence. At the same time, if we let them make and use swords, then it is our obligation to see that they do not get hurt. "I'm always anxious when a craze for wooden swords begins. I insist that the points be covered with rubber or cloth," says Neill. How much easier it is to simply prohibit children from playing with swords.

If Neill were to work in an American setting today, his actions would be very different from those described in *Summerhill* where the problems he deals with are so largely those of upper-class children. Not that things have changed as to what constitutes the right way to educate children, but much of the specifics have changed. For example, Neill tells us in *Summerhill* that: "Parents are spoiling their children's lives by forcing on them outdated beliefs; they are sacrificing their child to the past."

This statement is dated. What is permanent about it is that parents are warned not to sacrifice their children to their own neurotic anxieties. Today in the United States, I think the danger to middle-class children is that they are sacrificed by their parents not to the past, but to the future. Few middle-class American children suffer because authoritarian religion, against which Neill rages, is imposed on them. Instead, they are sacrificed by parents who burden them with the future, by telling them from early childhood of their need to correct the evils of the world. Other parents sacrifice their children to the future by insisting that if success later on in life is to be won the children must devote their present existence to preparation, and don the strait-jacket of competitive education.

In one sense, quite a few very liberal, well-educated, middle-class families, those most apt to believe they are raising their children in the philosophy of Summerhill, do sacrifice their children to the past. Not, as Neill suggests, by asking them to relive it, but by imposing on them the obligation to correct the errors of the past. Whether the child is burdened with reliving the past as it was, or burdened with reshaping the future, the child is being sacrificed to parental concerns. Too many parents fool themselves by assuming they believe in Neill's freedom, but do not grant their own child what Neill calls a child's most important privilege: the right to play in the present, that is, as I earlier quoted Neill, to play with guns at age ten. Instead, such parents ask their child to join at this age in their worries about the politics of the nation, and to do the work of the future.

Neill believes that to rear children well requires that "parents come to some sort of a compromise agreement; unhealthy parents either become violent [i.e., forcefully suppressive] or they spoil their children by allowing them to have all the social rights." And by forcefully suppressive, he includes the imposing of social or political convictions. Neill says, "A child cannot have real freedom when he hears his father's thunder against some political group." He recognizes that to give a child freedom is not easy, because "it means that we must refrain from teaching him religion, or politics, or class consciousness . . . I would never consciously influence children to become pacifists, or reformers, or anything else . . . Every opinion forced on a child is a sin against that child. A child is not a little adult, and a child cannot possibly see the adult's point of view."

This, I submit, is as true today as it was when Neill wrote it, and I wish that all liberal parents concerned with freedom would recognize how they deprive their children of freedom when they "thunder against" the inequities of our society, war, or the establishment. By thus raging against social inequities, justified as that may seem to the parent, they deprive their child of the most important thing of all: the right to form his own inner opinions, influenced not by the preachments of authority, but only by his own direct experience with life.

Neill does not "preach to children that slums are an abomination unto the world. I used to—before I realized what a humbug I was about it." The reason is not that slums are not an abomination—which they are—but that if we have failed to erase them, we have no business bothering our children with what is our problem, not theirs.

And the same goes for atomic war. "Today, even small children cannot help hearing about coming wars with the terrible atom bombs. But if there is no unconscious fear of sex . . . the fear of bombs will be a normal one . . . Healthy, free children do not fear the future. They anticipate it gladly." It is only when we impose on them our anxieties about the future (as of wars) that they come to fear the future and with it all of life. In this way, as Neill points out, we make them unhealthy because we force on them what he calls "the sick fear of tomorrow."

No doubt, we could and should be much more accepting of children's sexuality. But I do not share Neill's conviction that if only we could avoid all sex repression, encourage free sex play, particularly masturbation in children, all the evils of the world would dissolve, that there would no longer be hatred or wars.

Like his views about man, his views about sex derive directly from Reichean thought in the early days of psychoanalysis. Neill fails to consider the tendencies towards aggression which, according to students of animal behavior, are probably inborn in man, or certainly are a significant part of his makeup.

Believing, with some of our present social critics, in man's innate goodness, Neill concludes, as they do, that only sex-repressive (exploitative) society accounts for all the conflicts and contradictions we encounter in life. He ignores Freud's recognition that the greatest danger to human society does not come from repression, but from the instinct of aggression, from man's tendency towards destruction and self-destruction. In advocating complete sexual freedom, he does not concern himself with the fact that among pre-literate tribes where sex repression is very minor, man's anxiety is more pervasive, if anything; and in those societies, man must strive even harder to limit his anxieties through taboos and through what are often destructive rituals.

Neill also fails to consider that in such societies there is very little freedom in arranging one's life. Instead, all energy must go into securing a livelihood, since without repression, no higher forms of social organization are achieved, nor is that technology developed which alone protects us against sickness and famine.

I do not believe that man can live free of anxiety. For while it is true that anxiety brings about neurotic behavior, anxiety also brings about our highest achievements. All depends on how well we are able to sublimate these anxieties, how well we can set them to constructive use.

While Neill is excellent at reducing neurotic anxiety, he neglects what I consider the prime task of psychoanalytic education: to transform this force from one that shrivels us into a force that expands us and our lives.

In the same context, I think Neill errs when he thinks that

if a seven-year-old looks frightened at the sight of a cow and says, "No, no, moo cow eats you," it is because the child was brought up all wrong. Young children believe in the *lex talionis* however they are raised. Since we eat the cow's flesh, they believe the cow wants to eat ours, too. The source of such a belief is an inner anxiety, independent of sex repression, in which some of our own destructive tendencies find expression.

While I share Neill's concern about inhibiting masturbation and the bad effect of feeling guilty about it, I think he goes beyond the facts when he sees fire-setting as a consequence of the repression of masturbation. Freud's paper on the connection between fire and urination (phallic pleasure) should have taught Neill there is pleasure and excitement in setting fires and in watching them. While the sexual component in fire-setting is paramount, this is not due solely or mainly because of the prohibition of masturbation, or because of other sexual repressions.

Thus, while I do not doubt that children would be much better off if they enjoyed greater sexual freedom than most of them do, I question if the gain would be all Neill believes it would be if only we allowed our children total freedom in sex play. Certainly he is right when he says: "There would be infinitely less sex crime in the world if sex play [or sex in general, I would add] were accepted as normal." But this, too, has to be qualified in terms of what is age-correct; freedoms in this area, too, must be in line with man's normal growth and development. As much as freedom requires that the little boy should be free—free within himself, and free in terms of parental influence—to play with guns, and because of such freedom feel no need to concentrate his interest on them as an adult, so as a child he should be free to be interested in sex in line with what is then age-correct. He should be able to engage in masturbation without undue fear, but he should not need to do so provocatively, destructively, or excessively. He certainly should not concentrate on that at the expense of his interest and energy in social play, or at the expense of his relating to others. He certainly should not, as a child, engage in sexual intercourse. He should not need to use hetero-sexual relations as a substitute for masturbation, aggression, or upmanship. But compared with Neill's overall grasp of what children need for growing up well, as every page of his book testifies, these are small qualifications.

When it comes to the practical problem of how to deal with children and sexual issues, Neill is eminently sound. I could not agree more that it is "far better and safer to postpone an answer than to tell a child far too much" about sex, or at too early an age. Also that much of so-called sex instruction will not do because, as he says, "It's just a form of awkward lessons in anatomy and physiology."

Neill is also completely right when he says that what stops us from giving a child all the knowlege about sex that he asks for is the problem of how to make things clear. Neill might be writing of today when he says: "The modern parent may have no tempta-tion to follow that kind of [sex repressive] teaching, yet may succumb to something similar: the worship of the sexual function as a new-found god." Despite his theoretical over-valuation of sex freedom, in practice he realizes that to make too much of sex itself is also confusing to the child: "We all have been so condi-tioned about sex that it is almost impossible for us to see the middle, natural way; we are either too pro-sex or too anti-sex."

But it is not only in matters of sex that we push the children in terms of our anxieties, instead of understanding and accepting what is age-correct for them. Certainly it is destructive to the child to be induced to be competitive about his own education. Having just been criticized severely because I suggested that not everyone need go to college, and that many youngsters would

be much better off after going through high school or perhaps
even earlier, if they had been given a high level of training in
the professions or in special services, I was delighted to read:
"Over the years, we have found that Summerhill boys who are
going in for engineering do not bother to take the matriculation
exams. They go straight to practical training centers."

Here is a prescription that applies to all children, but especially at this moment in time, to many of our underprivileged
youth who could well use the chance to do what so many Summerhill boys do who "have a tendency to see the world as a ship's
steward."

Neill finds it just as destructive to the child to be induced to
cooperate at too early an age, as to be forced to compete. "There
is no case whatever for the moral instruction of children. It is
psychologically wrong. To ask a child to be unselfish is wrong.
Every child is an egoist and the world belongs to him. When he
has an apple, his one wish is to eat that apple. The chief result of
mother's encouraging his to share it with his little brother is to
make him hate the little brother. Altruism comes later—comes
naturally—*if the child is not taught to be unselfish*. It probably
never comes at all if the child has been forced to be unselfish."
But again, it is not quite as simple as Neill believes when he says
"there is no need whatsoever to teach children how to behave.
A child will learn what is right and what is wrong in good time—
provided he is not pressured."

The child will learn that only if he is surrounded by the right
human examples which are so attractive to him that he will want to
copy them, to shape his personality and values in the image of
those he admires and identifies with. But he will identify out of
anxiety, out of fear of losing the good will, or the presence, or the
respect of the loved person. There is no socialization nor any
learning without fear. Under primitive conditions or in a scarcity

economy, the fear is that we will starve if we do not learn how to gain our livelihood. In middle-class society, the fear, at first, is separation anxiety; then the fear of loss of respect of a person we love; and finally, the fear of loss of self-respect. Because what is right and what is wrong is nothing God-given, nor is it born with us, needing only unfolding.

On the other hand, children do have sufficient good sense to realize what is good for them and what is not, provided their own needs have been sufficiently satisfied to know what those needs are. "The truth seems to be that children take a much longer time to grow up than we have been accustomed to think. By growing up, I mean becoming a social being." And they become social human beings through experiences with other persons—not through experiences which do not involve anyone else.

It is these socializing experiences that Neill provided in all ways of life, by day and by night. This giving is what socializes the children—not their inborn nature, which is at best a potential to be realized through a great deal of living and learning. And the process takes time, much longer than we assume. That is why our push for early academic education often produces very bright but totally unsocialized persons, people who know a lot, but do not know how to live in a community of others.

But if the human example can do all that, children must not be overwhelmed, neither by our presence—which should be there to take or leave, but available when a child needs it—nor by our presents of which "children today get far too much, so much that they cease having appreciation for a gift." Children who have been given too much—be it toys, or academics, or stimulation, or the license to act without regard for others—are all spoiled children, unable to appreciate freedom, either their own or that of others. "Later in life, as the spoiled brat gets older, he has even a worse time of it than one subjected to too much discipline.

The spoiled child is terribly self-centered." This is a caveat to remember: that too little discipline may in the long run be more damaging than too much. If this is what experience has taught Neill of all people, we ought to heed his warning.

But the best discipline of all for the child is the self-discipline of the parent and the educator. This is the kind of self-discipline that prevents us from acting out on others our own anxieties and needs, certainly not on our children. This discipline permits us to be on their side instead of forcing them to be on ours. For things to work out to our liking, one's personal life should be of such nature that he would wish his child to emulate his life and take it as a model.

Neill's life and work are, indeed, such a model, even if we cannot agree with his theoretical formulations. Let us hope his followers will realize the facts and not try to set his philosophy into deadly practice, but rather to live as honestly and with as much respect for self and for others as Neill has in his long and enormously fruitful and satisfying life.

Holding academic credits from Cornell, Columbia, and Clark Universities, Eda LeShan in a long professional career, has been director of a number of associations dealing with family life and parent-child relationships. Her articles have appeared frequently in such magazines as PARENTS' MAGAZINE, THE NEW YORK TIMES SUNDAY MAGAZINE, REDBOOK, MCCALL'S *and* READER'S DIGEST.

She is the author of a number of books, among which the following are outstanding: HOW TO SURVIVE PARENTHOOD, THE CONSPIRACY AGAINST CHILDHOOD, *and* SEX AND YOUR TEENAGER, *and she makes frequent appearances on the national educational television program* NEWSFRONT.

Eda J. LeShan

It is a terrible thing to love a man you've never met; the only worse dilemma is to find yourself in fairly frequent disagreement with this man. This, in brief, is my problem with the father of Summerhill.

Having recently written a polemic against traditional education, I truly long to believe in the possibilities of a Summerhill for every child. Whatever the conceptual weaknesses of Summerhill may be, the profound humanity of Neill shines through his writing. No one in his right mind would doubt that Neill is one of the all-too-few genuine friends of childhood.

Yet assuming a tremendous amount of wisdom in Neill's ideas, why then, aren't there now successful Summerhill schools all over the world? The few that have tried to adopt his principles seem to be very poor imitations; in fact, many founder and die after a short while. Doesn't this constitute a serious judgment of Neill's work?

One part of the problem has been that so much of what Neill has written has been misunderstood. Is Neill's philosophy too subtle, too unworldly? What interferes with its wider application?

For some of us who are in general sympathy with the Summerhill philosophy, there are nevertheless flaws that might, indeed, preclude a wish for duplication. The first is Neill's continued loyalty to what some of us consider "old hat Freudianism." I sometimes suspect, as I re-read *Summerhill*, that Neill has been too busy living with children and loving children to have had sufficient time to modify his thinking in terms of newer insights and in terms of the broader perspectives that have developed over the past 25 or 30 years. Sexual repression is not exactly as crucial an issue today as it was in Freud's Victorian Vienna. In the past few decades there has been a great deal of clarification of how human beings operate. A sexual orientation is just simply too narrow a screen on which to view the entire scene of human motivation.

Another serious problem for those of us who sense Neill's over-all message but find it difficult of implementation is that he, himself, is so damned good at what he does that he tends to over-simplify his points. When Neill tells us how he would respond to a youngster's difficulties, he makes it all sound so easy. It probably *is* easy for him because his talents are somewhat larger than life-size, but his simplistic statements leave us in danger of believing that interactions between adults and children are quite uncomplicated. Few people are capable of Neill's intuition; and human beings happen to be terribly complicated.

But perhaps the greatest stumbling block to a full realization of Summerhill in other places is the undeniable fact that Summerhill stands isolated from the world in which most of us live; it seems to be a kind of magical and unreal island of enlightened human relationships—not like the churning, turbulent sea of human agony in which we labor and exist.

Right after World War II, a certain child psychiatrist came back to the States after serving as an Army doctor on Okinawa. He reported some marvelous observations he had made on that island. He had discovered that the children on Okinawa were remarkably placid and easy-going, almost fearless, and had an unusual tolerance for pain. He found no evidence of rivalry nor hostility among peers. In various articles and speeches, this doctor reported that he felt the "higher level of mental health" among the children of Okinawa was due to the fact that they were often nursed until the age of five, that they had experienced no coercive toilet training of any kind, and that the unconditional love and protective devotion of the entire community to its children provided them with a tremendous sense of security in the early years of their lives.

Around 1949, I heard this gentleman deliver a speech in Chicago. I recall how impressed I was with the movies he showed of the children submitting to painful surgical procedures with remarkable stoicism. However, after his speech, a child analyst in the audience stood up and said, "This is all quite fascinating, Doctor. But how do your findings relate to the child in the United States who has to fight for his life when some bully attacks him on the playground; and then, after he grows a bit older fight his way on to the subway to go to his high school where he has to fight and compete for good grades in order to get into college." That confrontation shocked me. I've never forgotten it.

In order for child-raising theories to _have significance, such theories must have application to the climate of life in which children live. We can't all go to Summerhill.

The question is can anything of Summerhill make children's lives in the decaying cities of the world more endurable? Can the ideas of Summerhill have meaning in this age of massive technology and population explosion, in this world of deepening anonymity and depersonalization?

Neill writes: "There must have been a time in the history of man when the fear of being killed made him flee and hide. Today, life has become so safe that fear in the service of self-protection is no longer necessary."[1] Not quite true, these days. Jungle fears have only been replaced by worse fears—fear of being knifed in the park in broad daylight, fear that some idiot might pull the wrong switch and blow us all to Kingdom Come, fear that our astronauts may bring back some insidiously infectious bugs from the moon, fear that some politicians would rather save face than

[1] p. 124, *Summerhill*

end an obscene and immoral war, fear of racial hatred and violence, fear of police action against young people. I'm sure that, today, Neill is aware of these realities. I find it hard to see how one can set as an educational goal the elimination of fear in a child's life, when for better or worse, this is *his* world, and there's fear in it. It may be that we must find ways to help a child sift out the different kinds of fear in his experience, and to learn how to tolerate what cannot be eliminated.

Another basic source of difficulty with Summerhill has been Neill's concept of palship between adults and children. A great many parents have experimented with this idea in a variety of ways over the past 25 years. While family life seems to me to have been greatly improved on the whole by the democratization of parent-child relationships, I think we have discovered that there are some important and realistic limits to such comraderie. There are many more choices open to us than either authoritarian discipline imposed through fear, or absolute personal autonomy for the child (provided he does not hurt or interfere with the rights of others.) For one thing, a young child has no background of experience for making choices; moreover, a child often cannot make the choice he knows is right because he is so much at the mercy of his childish impulses. A child cannot, it seems to me, be dumped out of his nest like a bird; he needs to make a great many test flights with strings attached before he reaches maturation. In a protected environment such as a boarding school, far more experimentation may be possible than in our society. In the enormously dangerous and complex urban centers where most children of today live, more limitations and safeguards are inevitable.

In the past few decades, child therapists have discovered that freedom by itself is not always helpful to the child. In the early days of psychiatry, rooms used for play therapy had to be rebuilt almost weekly as young patients vented their less lovely feelings by breaking down doors, smashing windows, stomping on toys, etc.

In recent years, therapists have tended to modify their early approach; they now permit a child to express his feelings to the point where it is clear what the child is communicating. But therapists have learned that a child is just as desperate for controls as he is for the opportunity to express his needs.

It is not enough to say that a child must only be stopped from doing what hurts others; he also wants to be stopped from doing those things that will make him feel ashamed of himself. Shame is not always, nor under all circumstances, an unhealthy or harmful feeling. If a child feels shame because he hasn't lived up to his own potential, that may be a useful experience. What is as harmful as Neill holds it to be is a child's developing self-contempt because of his failings. But here, too, there are subtle gradations. If an adult expects too little of a child, that in itself may produce feelings of unworthiness, just as clearly as too many pressures and expectations can produce baleful effects. Permissiveness carried too far will leave a child with too little pride in himself as a growing person. When an adult intervenes, it need not be to make a child feel that he is bad; it may, quite to the contrary, be a way of helping that child feel good about himself.

I know a case of an idealistic and dedicated student of social work who took a job as a neighborhood worker in the late 1940's. At that time, there were neighborhood gangs all over New York City, and social workers were assigned to "infiltrate"—that is, gain the confidence of the young people, try to direct their energies towards constructive activities, get them jobs, and generally serve as counselors. This young man, imbued with faith in gentle persuasion and the importance of personal freedom, decided that in order to help the members of his particular gang, he must first become a pal and live and think like one of the gang. So he started to gamble and swear, and he joined the boys in their drinking, and he never directly criticized them. He was very bewildered to discover that while the gang seemed to like him at first, their friendship cooled as time went on, and that they excluded him more and more from their activities. One night, he asked the leader of the gang to walk to the subway with him, and on the way, the counselor queried the tough as to what was going wrong. His young companion leveled with him and said, "The trouble is you're getting more like us, instead of us getting more like you."

It seems to me that the parents who have had the greatest success in raising their children are those who are reasonable, understanding, and loving, but who also *have made legitimate and realistic demands on their children,* so that the children see themselves as competent and successful, and quite capable of meeting the challenges and the demands that are made upon them in the world in which they live.

Some of us are too old and cynical for Neill's sweet belief in child nature. Neill writes "My view is that a child is innately wise and realistic."[2] Why should he be? Isn't the experience of living a large part of wisdom? Doesn't it make a difference whether a human being has or does not have a brain sufficiently completed to perceive reality? Although I am sure Neill doesn't mean to give this impression, a great many parents who read *Summerhill* come away with the feeling that children are innately and always innocent, good, lovable and *right*—that it is the parents who have all the neuroses, all the bad character traits, and who are a hopelessly confused, misguided, and not very intelligent lot.

I remember one parent discussion group where we were studying *Summerhill.* One mother, feeling very put upon stood up and

[2] p. 4, *Summerhill*

said, "I wish Neill would remember that I, too, was once a child—so how come I'm such a terrible person now?"

Another mother pointed out, "A lot of babies come into this world screaming and they want what they want the minute they want it. Then there are some babies who lie quietly and are sweet; and there are still other babies who get mad at you no matter what you try to do for them." This was a pretty smart lady because she said this about 20 years ago, during a time when just about all the experts had decided that environment was entirely responsible for the formation of a personality. There have since been some fascinating research studies that have reinforced what most alert parents have known along—that genes and chromosomes do *so* make a difference! The potential for all qualities, both lovable and revolting, are in all babies in very complicated and unequal proportions. Parents *do* have to take an active and decisive role in trying to direct the course these variations take.

In another discussion group, a mother talked about her twin girls, born within minutes of each other, nursed at the same breasts, twins who were different from each other from the beginning and who remained so, and had to be handled differently. At the time we met, the little girls were four years old. Their mother said, "From the first day, I knew they were completely different. One nursed easily; the other had a hard time getting started; one slept most of the time, the other fretted constantly. Just the other day I took them to a birthday party where they each got a box of crayons in which some of the crayons were broken. One of them was thrilled and said, 'Look, Mommy, two red ones and two green ones.' The other one howled bloody murder because the crayons were broken. Nobody's going to tell me that all babies are lovely and good, and that we ruin them!"

A baby screams and we say, "He's expressing a natural need." If a mother goes crazy listening to this screaming while struggling desperately but unsuccessfully to stop it and she finally screams back herself, that mother may become paralyzed with guilt. She feels judged; she has done something terrible. It seems to me that it would be far more helpful for parents and children to be encouraged to accept their common humanity, their common feelings and their imperfections—not to criticize just the parents for their vulnerability and frailty. A child can be a damned nuisance —unpleasant, mean, impatient, inconsiderate, and lazy. I would judge these characteristics to be by and large *human* characteristics, not always—nor even often—merely the results of bad handling on the part of parents.

Of course, there still are plenty of cruel and stupid people who do awful things to children. Neill and all the rest of us must rise up in our wrath against them. But today, there are also legions of parents who are trying desperately hard to be good parents, and who are greatly confused by complexities of freedom and permissiveness, and who need help to understand that they have an active and vital role to play in civilizing their children. The civilizing process won't just happen without adult guidance, without the imposition of reasonable limits, and without realistic demands and expectations.

The failure of ultra-permissive progressive education has been due not only to the strong demands such a system imposes on the teachers, but also because there are some children who, when given a great deal of freedom, tend to misuse that freedom. Some children do wonderfully in a free environment; somewhere in their germ plasm there is an inner control, an inner regulatory mechanism. These are the children who establish their own feeding schedules, toilet train themselves, and develop comfortable sleeping habits without outside discipline.

At the other extreme, there are children who are so innerly disorganized that they desperately need structure in their environment to keep them from constantly being in hot water with themselves and with other people.

There are some children who have so much energy and vitality and curiosity that if you placed them in an atmosphere where there were no formal classes in any subject, they would drain the brains of every adult around them, soaking it up like a sponge.

Then there are others, who even in a most exciting environment and surrounded by constant stimulation, might not attend any classes for 13 years.[3] Maybe the answer is that this type of child needs a different environment, different opportunities, different guidance—not in order for him to turn out the same as everyone else—but so that he may be able to utilize his particular qualities fully, and develop his own potential.

With so much emphasis today on academic achievement and the attainment of college degrees, what can we do for the child who doesn't want an academic education—who can't really use it? In Summerhill, such a child just doesn't go to classes. Hopefully, he eventually finds his own goals through his own self-directed activities. In the public school systems of the world at large, such a child sees himself as a total failure all the way through his schooling, and he suffers the tortures of the damned. He is coerced into studying totally irrelevant subjects that only continue to destroy every vestige of belief he might have in himself. Given such a choice, I'd surely rather have a child at Summerhill, but I do think there are other choices.

In the second half of the 20th century we decided—quite arbitrarily—that everyone had to be a thinker, and that we just didn't need any doers anymore. All children were to be educated as intellectuals; academic achievement was to be the only yardstick of human worth. Unfortunately, there is no such uniformity among

[3] p. 77, *Summerhill*

human beings. Some children love to learn from books; some need to learn through doing, from experiencing directly. What we need is an educational system that is open-ended—that doesn't set up impossible expectations and immutable standards. To that end, we need unstructured classrooms—at least in the early grades where we can watch how children begin to explore the world around them. From the reports that I have heard and read, it would seem to me that the Infant Schools of Great Britain represent a workable adaptation of Summerhill ideas.

However, a varied and flexible structure is not the same as no structure at all. The kind of facilities that can be provided in public education and the realistic limits of what communities are willing to invest in education mean that the large mass of schools cannot function with as much individual freedom for either adults or children as a private, experimental school. In addition to that practical reality, I believe that some expectations of the child are of value to the child. To expect nothing from a child may encourage him to expect nothing much from himself either.

Let me try to clarify what I mean by "not expecting much" of a child. Neill has a deep and abiding faith in all human potential. In that sense, he expects a great deal to emerge through normal development. On my part, I question whether the willingness to wait and to watch will not be interpreted by a young child as not caring about him.

There need not be any inevitable dichotomy—and Neill sometimes seems to be setting one up—between education aiming to produce a student who has accumulated much knowledge and many skills, and a student who is likely to grow up to be a happy individual. What seems more meaningful to me is to provide an environment in which a child is encouraged to involve himself in the task of exploring his own possibilities whatever these may be, but that he not be left alone to make this exploration mostly on his own. To evolve without direction is too difficult a task for some children; copping-out on oneself is too often the result.

For me, happiness seems irrelevant as a goal in itself. Happiness is one of those things that suddenly appears as a kind of piercing joy or a steady glow of good feeling when one is being most deeply and truly himself—most alive with one's own possibilities. Sometimes the most fulfilled person can be the most unhappy: the divine discontent of a brilliant mind and of a genuinely creative talent who always feels a sense of imperfection, who is always striving—and suffering!—never quite satisfied. That may be a marvelously productive way of life for certain individuals, although it isn't exactly a happy one.

Then there is the sensitive, loving person who is deeply troubled by man's inhumanity to man. He must be in the thick of things, struggling to change the world. He is rarely a happy person, but he has a deep sense of aliveness that seems to me to be a more legitimate and possible goal.

Neill sometimes gives the impression that it is better to give up the pursuits of the intellect in order to be a happy person; "a happy peasant rather than an unhappy scholar" is more or less the way he puts it. He says: "Books are the least important apparatus in the school."[4] I would modify that statement by saying, "Least important for doers; most important for thinkers."

Neill also tells us that the plays that are performed on Sunday night are almost always written by the children, occasionally by the teachers, but never by outsiders. It is true that there are children who learn about themselves and about other people through direct involvement, but on the other hand, there are other children of quite a different personality make-up for whom the ideas of others have far more significance in their growth. A child

[4] p. 25, *Summerhill*

shouldn't be obliged to abide by such a hard-and-fast choice—a child should be allowed to experience life in many different ways.

The gut issue in education today is not so much a question of happiness as the question of self-realization. Self-realization (or self-actualization) is one of the great goals of forward-looking educators. Dr. Abraham Maslow, past President of the American Psychological Association on leave from Brandeis University, has been largely responsible for the development of this new frame of reference. He represents a new breed who call themselves *Humanistic Psychologists*. This group may have great significance in propelling the ideas of Summerhill towards a new level of crystallization.

The struggle going on in educational circles today is far more dramatic, and its implications more momentous, than "to be or not to be happy." Neill really faces this more fundamental issue when he says, "It is a race between the believers in deadness and the believers in life. And no man dare remain neutral."[5] I see it as a struggle between mechanists and humanists; and Neill has most certainly been a humanistic Don Quixote knocking over the technological windmills long before most of us could even see them!

Mechanists and behaviorists view man as a very sophisticated machine; they are concerned with *in-put* and *out-put*, believing that if one can carefully control what one teaches and conditions, one will be able to predict—and direct—future behavior. Almost all *Rat Psychology* and *Learning Theory* has been based on a belief that the scientific method can make man predictable.

Behaviorism had its first development and recognition in the 1920's when Johns Hopkins psychologist, John B. Watson, following Pavlov's work on the conditioning of animals, held that if conditioning was used properly in infant and child care, a psychologist could predict what each child would become; he would even

[5] p. 103, *Summerhill*

be able to *plan* what such a subject would become. Watson's theories were a sorry failure; and some may have thought we had seen the end of this kind of simplistic view of the human experience. If we did, we underestimated the advancing forces of technology and the computerization of life. Behaviorism has returned with enormous force and today wields tremendous influence over much of psychology. Its chief spokesman is now B. F. Skinner of Harvard; wherever one turns, one finds Skinner's influence at work: in advice to parents on discipline through *Behavior Modification Theory,* and in such school achievement programs as that of Engelmann and Bereiter of the University of Illinois who have set about the tasks of "conditioning" our benighted black children into developing higher I.Q.'s. In general, behavioristic psychology represents the antithesis of everything Neill stands for.

Diametrically opposed to Skinner et al. are the *humanistic psychologists* led by Maslow. They are leery of applying the mechanistic method to the study of man, viewing this theory as an inappropriate tool in most instances. The humanistic psychologists tend to be profoundly moved by the wonder and mystery of human possibilities—they wish to enhance what is unpredictable about human beings, emphasizing the specialness of each individual. Where the approach of the mechanists depends on seeing man as a receiver of influences from outside his own skin, the humanistic orientation rests on the assumption that what a man may ultimately be is already potential within him from the moment of conception. The job of the educator, they hold, is to search for and elicit the rich and unique potential that is already there. The humanists have no interest in being able to predict behavior; their concern is with the process of *becoming,* the process in which each person discovers himself.[6]

[6] Abraham Maslow, *Toward a Psychology Of Being.* Van Nostrand, 1964

In this sense, the educator is a kind of gardener. He is a respecter of differences—fully aware that he cannot change a rose bush into a violet, and not the least bit interested in doing so. What concerns him is creating an environment where a rose bush can become its best rose-bush-self—and where a violet can become its best violet-self. This point of view has been beautifully expressed by John Holt:[7]

> *We can think of ourselves not as teachers but as gardeners. A gardener does not 'grow' flowers; he tries to give them what he thinks will help them grow, and they grow by themselves. A child's mind, like a flower, is a living thing. We can't make it grow by sticking things onto it any more than we can make a flower grow by gluing on leaves and petals. All we can do is surround the growing mind with what it needs for growing, and have faith that it will take what it needs and grow.*

It seems to me that the humanistic psychologists have made a very real contribution to education. While they remain within the philosophical framework of Summerhill, they have already moved us a step or two beyond Neill's approach. For example, Maslow speaks of a *third force* in psychology and education. He speaks of this as "The doctrine of the Real Self to be uncovered and actualized." In such a frame of reference, "The job of the psychotherapist or the teacher is to help a person find out what's already in him, rather than to reinforce him or shape him or teach him in a prearranged form which someone else has decided upon in advance."[3] In this approach, the teacher must be somewhat less

7 Redbook Magazine, November, 1965
8 Abraham Maslow, *Some Educational Implications of the Humanistic Psychologies.* Harvard Educational Review, Fall, 1968, 38,#4.

passive than the Summerhill teacher who waits for the child's invitation to give out instruction. Maslow suggests that the teacher should play a very active role in "uncovering or discovering . . . the way in which you (the child) are different from everybody else in the whole world."

Maslow also discusses two kinds of learning: *Extrinsic Learning* and *Intrinsic Learning*. He describes *Extrinsic Learning* as learning from the outside, learning of the impersonal, learning through arbitrary associations and conditionings. In this type of learning, rarely does the learner decide what he will learn; he is coerced into accumulating associations, conditionings, habits, that become his "possessions." This kind of learning has little or nothing to do with the special, unique qualities of the learner. It is the kind of learning fostered by the mechanistic approach. The teacher is active, the student passive—a receptor to be shaped and taught. The student accumulates what he is given, and he may lose that or retain that, depending on the efficiency of the indoctrination process, and depending on his own responsiveness. Such learning reflects the goals of the teacher, and largely ignores the values and goals of the learner. This kind of learning is characteristic of about 90% of the kind of teaching experienced by most children—a learning associated with drill and repetition in the learning of specific skills and in the memorization of facts. The teacher is a lecturer, a conditioner, a reinforcer—a boss.

Intrinsic Learning, unfortunately, occurs almost exclusively *outside* the classroom. It is partly unconscious. It is the kind of learning that takes place in psychotherapy, and is the kind of learning that goes on as a human being lives through the significant events of his life—getting married, having children, facing the death of a friend or parent. There is no drill and there is no repetition. (Maslow asks, "How do you repeat the death of your father?"). These are the experiences through which we learn *who* we are, *what* we love, *what* we hate, *what* we value, and through which we discover our identity. These experiences have to do with learning to be a person. This is surely the kind of learning Neill is concerned with. In *Intrinsic Learning*, the teacher is a helper, a counselor, a guide. His job is to help a child learn what kind of person he already is—his style, his aptitudes, and his potentialities are explored together. In such learning, there can be genuine enjoyment of one's own growth and one's self-actualization. In this formulation, one acknowledges differences more directly. Self-actualization rather than happiness becomes the fundamental goal.

Neill's greatest contribution to education has been to be in the vanguard of those humanizing forces now represented by the *humanistic psychologists*. It matters not one wit whether or not there are any successful copies of Summerhill as a school. If we were to value Summerhill only as it could be reproduced in facsimile, we would be missing the main point. We would be looking for easy answers that Neill has not promised and cannot deliver.

I hardly need to document the interest, excitement, and inspiration that Neill has aroused all over the world. However, I think there is one current phenomenon that is rarely connected with his philosophy and teachings, and about which I think Neill might well take some pride and credit. For, above all, Neill has had a profound influence on my generation as parents—and I think his influence has showed up in the behavior of our young people.

It has occurred to me that in the past year or so many of Neill's ideas have come to realization in the young rebels on our college campuses. To those who think these youngsters are dirty, undisciplined, irresponsible, and immoral, the contemporary crop of campus rebels must seem to be living proof of the failure of permissiveness. But I find these boys and girls the most idealistic young people ever raised by any generation. They care nothing for material comfort nor for security; they cannot endure hypocrisy; they are not the least bit fooled by superficial appearances; they are deeply honest and absolutely color blind as far as race is concerned. They have enormous insight into themselves, and have great compassion for others. But what is most fascinating is that they seem free of most of the neurotic expressions of anger. The only thing they are really angry about is social injustice.

It seems to me that my generation of parents—now in their mid or late forties or in their early fifties—raised a generation of giants. I am surprised that we did it, but we disciples of Freud and Spock and Neill and Dewey seem to have brought up a generation of young people who *really* believed all the things we told them when they were little. We talked about the brotherhood of man, and we declaimed about the shallowness of judging people by outward appearances. We certainly talked about the hopelessness of war as a solution to international problems. What surprises us out of our minds is that these children *listened,* and that they actually want to *practice* what we merely *preached!* How did they get that way?

What intrigues me is that Neill's idea of freedom helps children to grow up without hate. I think our adolescents have demonstrated the soundness of this theory. They were allowed more freedom to think and to feel than any previous generation of children. We gave them a great deal of psychological insight into human motivation; and they were able, with unbelievable facility, to search out the hidden meanings in their own and in other people's behavior. Because of this, they have felt less anger at themselves, and have experienced less need to focus anger upon others. Instead of developing psychosomatic diseases or looking for scapegoats, they have gotten plain mad about human suffering.

We seem to have helped our children avoid a good deal of self-hatred; they really *are* "love children"; they love where it counts—in interpersonal relationships.

Instead of rejoicing in this miracle, we hit them over the head with clubs. But Neill ought to be triumphant about these young people on the barricades. Most of them came from democratic households; they are the first generation who was raised with more kindness than fear, more understanding than punishment.

An interesting commentary about this phenomenon recently appeared in *Today's Child* (April, 1969) in a report of a meeting held in Rome and sponsored by the Vatican and the University of California at Berkeley on "The Culture of Unbelief." The question was why are there so many atheists among young people today?

An interesting side issue emerged. Dr. Peter Berger, a sociologist at The New School for Social Research in New York, suggested that children who had had a relatively happy childhood were mostly concerned with humanizing society and were not concerned with metaphysical matters. He said that such children want to make society more closely resemble their own childhood. He said that "Youngsters who have had comparatively happy childhoods may be more sensitive to suffering when they finally see that it exists, and may be less likely to accept inhumanity and cruelty as man's lot . . ."

For those of us who are encouraged by the presence of young social rebels among us, Dr. Berger's statement is, indeed, an encouraging indication of the possibilities inherent in enlightened child-raising procedures.

The simple fact of the matter is that Neill finally comes through as one of the great artists of our time in how to be a beautiful human being. In his reverence for life, his sense of the sacredness of human personality, he is a true gardener of childhood. Neill says—far too humbly, I think—that he sees his job as "not the reformation of Society, but the bringing of happiness to some few children." [9] From this onlooker's point of view, it seems that just

9 p. 23, *Summerhill*

the opposite is true. That Neill has helped a handful of children to feel good about themselves as human beings is nice, but that is really incidental from a long range view. What is far more important is that we can never be the same after knowledge of his dream.

I have come to the conclusion that a great teacher can never be successfully imitated. It would be pointless to ask Picasso to give us lessons so that we could paint as he does. We cannot ask to be taught that. What a great artist in any field can do is INSPIRE— show us something, new or old, in a special light that profoundly helps to express our own deepest feelings.

I recall my sense of shock many years ago when my husband was studying at the University of Chicago. I had just been reading Carl Rogers, and I was exhilarated and inspired by his brilliant insights and wonderful compassion. Then I had occasion to meet some of his disciples and in some cases, their therapeutic procedures were so terrible they were not to be believed. I'm sure this kind of thing accounted for much of the strife and turmoil in Freud's life. Geniuses can't teach other people to be geniuses— all they can do is provide marvelous new insights, and breadth of perspective.

Inspiration is the heart of the matter. If Neill inspires teachers and parents to care more deeply, look more carefully and sensitively, and seek out better ways to educate humanity, that is quite enough. The rest is up to us.

Michael Rossman is an outstanding representative of today's left wing campus, and has been involved in most of the youth political action in the Bay area.

For the past two years, Mr. Rossman has been active as a campus organizer, agitator, and trainer in the youth movement. As he puts it, he is "largely by default, the leading theoretical writer in the youth educational reform movement, but would rather write poems. At this sad point in history, most of your readers would probably recognize me most accurately as a maniac dope fiend anarchist freak, for I have no particular institutional identity. I do, however, have publications which provide me with a resulting image of solidity." Some of these are: THE MOVEMENT AND EDUCATIONAL REFORM (THE AMERICAN SCHOLAR), BLACKS AT MAINSTREAM U (COMMONWEAL), THE TWO FACES OF YOUTH (SATURDAY REVIEW), NOTES FROM A CALIFORNIA JAIL (NEW YORK REVIEW).

Mr. Rossman received his A.B. from Berkeley in 1963, which he followed with four years of graduate work. He worked with the San Francisco State Experimental College in 1966, and assisted Dr. Harold Taylor in a study of teacher training in 1967, concentrating on the interaction of education and politics.

Michael Rossman

In *Summerhill*, A. S. Neill examined not freedom—whose song he sings with random gladness and confidence—but authority. He described the coercive quality of what he calls "imposed authority"—authority exerted through punishment, reward, and shame, and involving the repression of natural energies and anger. For the hate and crippling that result from this kind of authoritarian rule, Neill sketched therapies of trust and love, of release of what has been held back, and of living-out of what has been denied. In opposition to imposed authority, Neill sought the development of "self-regulation" which far from controlling, permits and aids growth. So Neill built an insular learning community organized around the freeing authority of self-rule. In this isolated laboratory called Summerhill, he studied how and what children learn when they are free to learn, and wrote his observations into a book.

Summerhill's importance should be measured less by the tributes of educators and by the fact that it has been widely adopted as a college text, than by its popularity among America's young. Hundreds of thousands have read Neill's simple clear prose, and have embraced his thought in their own. As nearly as can be in this age of rich and multiplying influences, Neill will become the Dr. Spock of these generations of "post-modern" young just now maturing into parenthood. For Neill entered their minds at a fortunate time: when they were on the verge of new growth, in a fertile climate of experiment and longing. Intimately involved with movements for the self-determination of all peoples, this generation responded with quick sympathy to Neill's essay on raising free children.

For the post-modern young adults were born into a culture dominated by pathological authoritarian control. In America, authority is typically exercised as a function of fixed and centralized roles in an hierarchical system. The face of this authority is always benevolent, but its underlying power lies in coercion, within a framework of punishment and reward. The authority system controls energy and controls change to satisfy its own needs—in particular, the need to preserve the status quo of power and above all, to ensure that *its* own nature and form are not changed. The consequence is always some form of cultural imperialism in which the identity of what is controlled tends to become an image of the authority.

These features of what I will call the *Authority Complex* are visible throughout our systems of education, parenthood, social organization, and international politics. America knows no other style. And since learning and social change are complementary processes, the Authority Complex sabotages both. For change through self-regulation depends on functional skills: on the individual's ability to formulate problems and set goals, on his ability to identify the resources available in the total social environment, on his ability to create procedures, and to establish valid criteria. As shown by the example of classroom teaching in most schools today, these functions are pre-empted by the Authority Complex, and the basic skills of autonomous learning are generally stunted in their development.

Moreover, the very essence of learning is violently distorted. For if learning be thought of as a conversation—not limited to words on either the social or the personal level—then its key subconversation is an interaction among the participants about the goals and the processes of their development. But the Authority Complex sets severe limits on this conversation, in order to restrict the intellectual, psychological, and social constructs to which change may lead.

Now America's young are in the midst of a broad change, whose causes are still poorly understood but whose nature is clear. They are learning to undo the crippling effect of the Authority Complex through a many-leveled system of education that, on a large scale, resembles Neill's experiment in freedom. Their learning includes intense and unsanctioned experiences outside the classroom walls: the politics of confrontation and liberation, the therapeutic community of the white ghettos whose prototype was Haight-Ashbury, the varieties of psychedelic experience, as well as a new music and culture which have generated forms like "underground radio," and new group forms, like *be-ins*. Their alternative education also includes the spontaneous development of free learning groups now organized into some 800 "free universities." Whatever the medium, the result is the flowering of free children who are able to develop their selves and their loves.

* * *

In *Summerhill*, Neill describes many of the phenomena of healthy growth. All depend on the development of an alternate style of shared, democratic, and flexible authority, whose power is exercised through example rather than by coercion. Such authority empowers rather than weakens those exposed to it.

As Neill observed, growth within a freeing authority is richly diverse and untidy, as in the Haight-Ashbury or in free universities. There are no uniform norms. Growth proceeds by the unblocking of repression, and through the therapy of living out deep, immediate energies and needs. The clearest examples of this process are the deconditioning experiences of psychedelic drugs and the political conflicts on our campuses. When freed from coercive authority, the young create a radical democracy, a non-coercive peer society which depends on mutual approval and trust, and whose native values are sharing, honesty, gentleness, and tolerance for the wide range of people's real natures. Such a Summerhillian society is now appearing wherever the free young practice their changes.

Neill teaches one to love himself. *Summerhill's* preoccupation with masturbation is more symbolic than substantive; for us the motions of self-love are more aptly described as "de-niggerization." For America makes niggers of all her children by the reigning processes of the Authority Complex. Our systems of learning and life, governed by punishment and shame, teach us to dislike ourselves and to distrust our capacities. A deep anger gathers which fear does not permit us to express directly, an anger which sours into a hate of the flesh. The conjugate voice of love is stilled as well, souring into greed. People, so trained, find it difficult to believe in each other enough to learn from each other, or to create healthy change.

The first problem in building a revolutionary movement or a learning group is to get people to take themselves seriously, to believe in their own beauty and dignity, and in their collective power.

Touched off by a psychic contagion from the blacks, a broad process of deniggerization is spreading through America's white young, many of whom have been newly freed to develop personal and cultural identity. Literally millions are coming to think proudly of themselves as "freaks," a term reflected in the acid motto "Freak freely!" To freak freely is to fully let out, to fully live in the energies repressed by our society. All the media of alternate education in America now partake in this process of young people learning to love the beauty of their dark selves.

*   *   *

But the cry, "Black is Beautiful!" takes us beyond Neill's teachings, if not beyond his observations. For as Franz Fanon observes, for a colonized people violence is necessary in the formation of a new identity. True, Neill recognizes the need to act out the over-throwing of parental authority. But Neill does not deal with the broader consequences of such behavior. "My primary job," he says, "is not the reformation of society, but the bringing of happiness to some few children." He limits his perspectives.

But, of course, the happiness of many children and the revolution of society as a whole are at stake; and these two constitute a single task. Neill is emphatic about the need to consider growth, as it occurs in a total context, and he is clear about the limits of his own experiment. Summerhill is his insular preserve. Attached to the larger, anti-life society only by umbilical dependence on supportive parents, Summerhill is not forced into direct conflict to provide space for its own happening.

America's young, however, are not so fortunate. Only some few can be made happy in the little space now free. Their histories testify that in order to clear space for self-regulated growth one must inevitably come into conflict with the forces of repression. A struggle against the full breadth of the social organization will ensue. Since the isolated therapy-center called Summerhill was, ab initio, a free space, Neill had no need to focus on the tools of change, or on the methods required to overthrow inappropriate government. His goal was to create learner-citizens, rather than revolutionaries.

But significant learning or change in human systems is always explicitly revolutionary: it involves the death of one order and the creation of another. Whether the change be the elimination of racism, or the learning of a mathematical theorem, or the finding of love, or the cancellation of conditioning that gives priority to women and to authority figures, what is involved is always the disruption and death of an organic system, and the birth of a new order. That birth may become easier if the revolutionary aspects are better understood.

*   *   *

If learning *is* revolution, then the goal of education should not be the acquisition of a degree, but the creation of a healthy *process* and its attendant skills. This involves three main factors: (1) learning to break free from old and crippling frameworks of control; (2) learning to build in the freedom created; (3) learning to think about the process of change itself. Of these, Neill deals with the first two in gentle and fragmentary remarks—remarks, however, that do not testify, as all the major learning experiences of my generation do, to the difficulty of creating and enduring the *chaos* of freedom in which growth occurs.

Sometimes the form of open space is tangible: a group of persons newly met together; a new social or artistic form; a vacant lot. More usually, open space is a matter of seeing *differently*, seeing *newly*. Any new technology induces its corresponding area of consciousness. So does a personal contradiction or a social contradiction. Such contradictions are openly revealed when the conflict between a system's operations and its actual needs grows critical. Exposure to new behavior breaks our limits of expectation. Examples of change expand the universe of possibility.

To open new consciousness is to "blow the mind." The conjugate patterns of behavior and cognition are broken. Space is freed from the control of old and decadent logic. The authorities of closure must be removed, counteracted, or broken by conflict. The alternate education of America's young is rich in examples of such anti-authoritarian processes, and of the open spaces that result. In particular, the psychedelic experience and confrontation politics give clear models of the mechanisms of "mindblowing." In general, personal and social conflict are overt, for behavior that truly reduces the control and threatens the existence of the Authority Complex is not likely to go unnoticed or uncountered.

To open space for free growth involves dealing directly with anger and fear. The example of demonstrators waiting in the theater of their emotion for the police to descend upon them with clubs and guns is typical. To engage these emotions fully is deeply therapeutic. Observers of campus conflict are familiar with the heavy charges of anger and fear, with the enormous amounts of energy liberated in the participants, and with the striking efficiency of the translation of that energy into productive work.

This work is personal as well as social. For a sense of public, collective empowerment carries over into the private domain, and public behavior that shatters conventional expectations creates psychic space in the form of new vistas for personal potential. It is because of this relationship between personal growth and the successful experience of anger that the recent political movements among the blacks and the white young are so strongly connected to the broader movements of cultural change that are spreading in their wakes.

* * *

But anger and fear must be dealt with—not once to free space—but constantly, to maintain the freedom of the new space. For every act of learning involves a crossing into unknowable space, not yet fully structured into order. To face the unknown is to embrace incoherence: it invokes a primal fear of chaos. Fear of the known is specific, and can be dealt with cleanly. Fear of the unknown is the central psychological problem of all learning; its conjugate expression is the use of power to control and to prevent change, which is correctly anticipated as the death of a system.

Such fear is seen clearly in the inability of most teachers to help create the new relationship and interactions that students are learning to demand. In general, the faculties have responded with simple, deep terror.

* * *

There are supports against the fear of chaos. The spectrum is seen most compactly in the psychedelic experience, which for the young, now outclasses personal therapy in providing an arena in which fear may be investigated in depth, without immediate dangerous social consequence.

First there is the fear of breaking social law. This fear is reduced by intimate embedding in a smaller peer society which sanctions psychedelic use and demonstrates its value. But there are endless layers of the onion of inner fear. After entering space essentially unknown, progress is measured directly by the peeling of these layers. From outside, the tools for moving through fear consist mainly of peer support and knowledge about the process and its phases; from inside, the supports derive from a series of spiritual disciplines.

The rituals of psychedelic use are functional sacraments: they are rituals of beginning, of entrance into a community of shared learning. These rituals are the most public of the simple human transactions of trust so important in dealing with the emotions of the processes of change.

The society of psychedelic use is one of self selection. It espouses an ethic of sharing; it is a community of brothers openly—and successfully—struggling with the processes of their learning. In such a community, fear is dramatically reduced. In this climate failure is not only openly accepted, but failure is attended by deep support. People learn to trust their emotions, their rhythms, and their common sense.

In all these regards, the society of psychedelic use resembles Summerhill. Such a society furnishes a general model for the frameworks of trust that must underlie any healthy community of learning. Because such a society is centrally concerned with opening mysterious and dangerous space, the phenomena of touching and trust in this society are particularly characteristic of all current alternate education which America's young are undergoing in their free schools, new politics, and ghetto communities.

Psychedelic use also illuminates the technologies of relaxation, of *letting go*. Anxiety is the great magnifier of fear, and derives from and leads to the blocking of psychic energies. Anxiety thrives on *IF*. But psychedelic use conditions one to live more intensely in one's actual experience. (In general, the acceleration of social change now leads the young to live increasingly in the present.) The mind's inner authorities—from logic to suger-ego— are decompulsified by the psychedelic experience. The anxiety that knowledge, action, and experience itself be immediately coherent within a known framework seems to give way. Instead, a sense of esthetics emerges which admits mystery, incoherence, and sudden change as central values.

Psychedelic use makes evident the need for disciplines to deal with freedom. Mostly such disciplines are best described as spiritual: they teach the skill of letting go anxiety, of *being* in one's being—or, equivalently, the renunciation of coercive power and control. Such disciplines yield the reward of increased ability to draw strength from one's being, and to draw nourishment from one's partially-successful changes. In yoga, meditation, and Zen, the young are increasingly investigating such disciplines. From a simpler psychological viewpoint, the disciplines depend on repeated encounters to develop a tolerance of the unknown.[1] But beyond tools and skills, there is always necessary that act of the will which faces fear itself ever more directly.

* * *

A second main component of free growth with which Neill does not deal adequately is anger. Though *Summerhill* often refers to

---

[1] Not surprisingly, cross-cultural experience provides deep training and models for change, especially in regard to therapies for fear of the unknown. The best model I know of self-regulated learning is provided in a study on preparing people to teach within other cultures. See Roger Harrison, "The Design of Cross-Cultural Training: Alternatives to the University Model," in *The Changing College Classroom*, Runkel, et. al. eds., (Joosey-Bass, 1969.)

anger, Neill treats anger as if it can be worked through once and then be done with, as if it were not an essential constant in the act of learning. But if the birth of new knowledge is the death of old systems and limits, then anger is intrinsic to the process, for no system dies in tranquility.

Our own time and culture generates another anger. Unable to change, we translate our frustrated need into a general hatred and murder. Within my lifetime, the main stream of Western literature and art has turned to a rich expression of powerless agony, watching a dying culture race to work out the death of our species. The increase in crime and the cry of the literati and the artist are but two of the cultural barometers that register our burden. These barometers warn starkly that we do not know how to build social or personal forms and processes which deal adequately with our anger. Instead, we act out our anger uncontrollably, and generate the continual helpless violence which is America's grossest national product.

For many years, the peace of the American classroom has been the silence of frustration and the boredom of death. Since 1964, an enormous charge of righteously hateful anger has begun to be acted out against the established systems of education. Such anger does not simply vanish in the alternate educational systems the young are developing. Experience throughout the free universities proves that when people come together to replace authority-centered learning with the style of a self-regulated group, the participants must deal with stored up and unexpected anger—not only initially, but at each junction of decision.

The child's first cry from out of the blackness is of anger and fear. Through them he enters into the chaos of a new world, to begin the act of learning. The will to live transforms his anger and fear into the aggression that powers growth. However it goes, I know that today anger and fear must be dealt with in the act of learning. And the proper governance of anger requires more machinery than tolerance.

That machinery is built by bootstrapping up from almost nothing. A small group cultivates a consciousness of the process of its learning, a consciousness which recognizes the constant presence of anger and the need to deal with it. As a beginning, the group establishes norms of openness to permit the expression of anger. Beyond this, skills for the government of anger must be deliberately developed.

To give one example: in a work-group, the larger work-processes become stifled by accumulated anger among the participants. The group unlocks this anger by recognizing it, and shifting to a therapeutic sub-process: the group breaks up into couples which act out several cycles of anger and aggression and reconciliation in non-verbal mirror games. Then they resume their work. Analagous tools are being developed on a larger social scale.

If I seem unduly concerned with chaos and its content, that is because my native culture denies these and other mysteries. Yet the live face of chaos is one with the existential crisis of freedom and choice. The crises of encounter and confrontation open rich social and psychological space. When it denied chaos, our culture was forced to provide a substitute, and it chose the tools of coercion.

Our consumer economy now largely derives from the technology of the Warfare State. Every student's productive life will depend heavily on his ability to use in tomorrow's test the skills desperately learned tonight. But there must be a better way. Death is the message of every closed system. To survive, we must enter unknown free territories.

*   *   *

As Neill recognizes, the skills of interest are the ones we do not have, or cannot properly use. Our institutions efficiently condition us in some skills of the mind and of social response—especially those skills which impose the strictures of operating within limits. Our problem is to learn to use these skills as tools rather than as tyrannies. The psychedelic experience is a model for such deconditioning. It restores a balance between competing skills—between the ability to defer and the ability to accept gratification.

In most alternate education, students come together to decide what they want to learn, and to learn *how* to learn it. To learn is to go on. Each member's goal is to be able to lead the group ahead when that is appropriate, and also to facilitate the learning process for others. His share of authority begins with his knowledge of the state of his learning, and of his skill in helping others to change. Such authority provides a common denominator of leadership in a group whose concern is mutual participation. Each participant must perceive himself, as well as the others of his group, as responsive to *change*—rather than as players of stereotyped roles which rigidly limit the possibilities of growth. In the conversation of such a group, as much emphasis is given to the *process* of its learning as to the content of that learning. Such balance is simply impossible in authority-centered learning. For to deal well with difficulties in process involves a challenging of the Authority Complex.

The consciousness of process in learning has its analogue on the larger social scale in the form of a *reflexive institution*. Such an institution has within itself explicit mechanisms for consciously examining the state and processes of its growth, and for changing itself in response to this learning. One common example is the free university. It is critical to note that such a reflexive core is neither a study group nor an element of a check-and-balance system. In a free university, all energies of the free university are marshalled into self-directed change; and participation is open to everyone. By contrast, compare the standard mechanisms for change in most of today's American colleges.

In order to survive in this age of accelerating change, all personal and social systems must in some sense contain mechanisms for their own continuous change. The process of change is now so rapid that we are forced to relate to change itself as a phenomenon. No culture in history has ever been called upon to develop mechanisms whose function is to render healthy the process of change itself. Our civilization does not display, at present, much evidence of self-changing capacity. Our present modes of politics are completely inadequate. When they do reveal information about our process, there is no consequent action. For example, within the Departments of Psychology of our universities, experiments have long proven that our system of testing and grading assesses—not knowledge nor learning skills—but the success of conditioning. Yet that system of punitive evaluation continues as the dominant motivational framework for learning. What will it take, short of a million Summerhills or short of total revolution, for us to be able to *apply* our knowledge to our goals?

The alternate education of the young in America now tends to the creation of a radically new order. Process-consciousness must, I think, involve the full forms of participatory democracy. What is required is radical decentralization of structure and of power—an imperative now clearly faced by our cities, as well as by our culture in general. This decentralization has its interior analogue in the process of learning; to let all of one's voices, without words, have their say.[2] This would seem to require a taste for chaos and

---

[2] One current aspect of this process is the investigation by the young of decision-making tools from other or earlier cultures—the *I Ching*, astrology, the Tarot, etc. These investigations provide information about the internal states of the decision-making system. Such tools are an essential element of process-consciousness.

The changes of our century are carrying us back to the tools and knowledge of earlier cultures, especially to metaphysics like Taoism which deal directly with the phenomena of change.

incoherence.

The construction of a conversation with *no* limits, always instantly open to new elements, is clearly a convenient fiction. In order to build, limits must continually be generated. But the imposition of such limits must come from *within,* not *without;* and be ever again broken, in a rhythm of eternal and self-regulated revolution.

We have no choice about that cycle. We can only learn to tend the health of its rhythm. At the present time, that compels us more to make revolution than to prevent it.[3]

---

[3] The subjects treated in this essay are dealt with in considerably more detail in a series of papers, "On Learning and Social Change, Parts I, II, and III," available from the Center for Educational Reform of the National Student Association (2115 S Street N.W., Washington, D.C. 20008); and also beyond those papers in more depth in my book *Making The Changes,* forthcoming from Doubleday in 1970.

Author of some 50 books, monographs, and articles on psychology and juvenile delinquency, Dr. Ernst Papanek occupies the post of Professor of Education at the City of New York University at Queens College.

He studied pediatrics and psychiatry at the Medical School of the University of Vienna. He received his doctorate in education at Teachers College at Columbia University in 1934.

In 1938, Dr. Papanek organized and directed the children's homes and experimental schools of the Organisation pour la Sante et l'Education in France. After he made his home in the United States, he became Executive Director of the Brooklyn Training School for Girls in 1947, and then Executive Director of the Wiltwyck School for Boys in 1949. Here, his experiments in the re-education of juvenile delinquents have resulted in his becoming a nationally known figure in this area.

Ernst Papanek

*"Abolish authority. Let the child be himself.
Don't push him around. Don't teach him. Don't
lecture him. Don't elevate him. Don't force him
to do anything."*

Thus one of my graduate students started her introduction to
a class discussion about Summerhill. She then continued:

*"That is A. S. Neill's advice on how to insure
our children's happiness. Neill's school, Summerhill, allows children freedom to discover life on
their own, without imposition of society's many
guilt-motivated or hate-motivated values. The
Summerhill idea is that the child must find happiness, and a happy streetcleaner is better off than
an emotionally disturbed professional."*

Summerhill is read and discussed in all my classes at Queens
College. Before offering my own views, I would like to present
some excerpts from the reports and the discussions of students,
most of them very favorably impressed by Neill's thinking; some
of them doubtful; still others, sarcastic.

One student declares:

*"Summerhill is not interested in job-training,
political awareness, nor in altruistic behavior.
This is because Summerhill is not out to produce
adjusted citizens, but adjusted men. But an ad-*

*justed man turns out to be an adjusted citizen.
Neill is more interested in letting the individual
develop on his very own terms.*

*"Hence, I could never bring up a child in the
Summerhillian way even if I thought the system
had merit. For Neill is preparing children for life
in some possible future society, certainly not
for life in our actual society."*

"No!" I interpolate "Neill is preparing children for life as independent individuals, but not for life as happy members of society."

*"Similarly, Neill's notion of punishment is a bit
hazy. On page 167, he tells the story of a boy
who hit and bit him. To teach him that such behavior was wrong, Neill hit the boy back every
time he received a blow. I erroneously came to the
conclusion that he favored the old eye-for-an-
eye doctrine; but later in the book, Neill speaks
disapprovingly of those misguided parents who,
when trying to teach Junior not to stick baby
with a pin, stick Junior with a pin so that he will
know how that feels."*

Another points out:

*"Try as I may, I cannot understand Neill's
position about fear. His reasoning seems to be
circular. On page 124, he states: 'Fear must be
entirely eliminated . . . Only hate can flourish
in an atmosphere of fear.' I immediately thought
about the possibility of eliminating all fear. I*

*wonder what state the world would be in if no-
body feared anything or anyone?*

*"Then on page 127, Neill makes a distinction
between anxiety and fear, adding that fear is
necessary or 'we should all be run down by buses.'
Well, where does he stand?*

*"As a matter of fact, it is anxiety that we
should try to do away with."*

Another commentator offers:

*"In an atmosphere of freedom, either at home
or in school, each individual should be allowed
to do whatever he likes, as long as he does not
infringe on the freedom of others. Neill main-
tains that children and adults have equal rights.
'When a child tells me to get out of his room, I
get out,' he says. 'The child must also leave my
room when I ask him to leave.'"*

I can't help commenting in this regard that it seems to me that
Neill's is negative thinking. I, for one, would rather talk of equal
rights of invitation, each asking the other to visit his room. Neill's
ideas of freedom are out-dated. Who is to decide when and where
one freedom should be limited by another freedom? What we
need is social interest in each other: constructive, positive community feelings, and an assumption of responsibilty. We *must* become our brothers' keepers.

Says another class discussant:

*"Neill believes in the self-regulated child; let
the youngster play and plan and dream and*

dream, for when that boy is ready to learn, he will attend class because he wants *to learn.*

"But what about the slow late learner who might have become, under proper stimulus, a great leader? Is he to go down the drain?

"Neill says: 'Parents interpret self-regulation in so many different ways, sometimes bringing disaster to the child.' If that is so—and I believe it is—the impracticability of his methods condemn them. There are just too few Neills.

"Neill believes young children should be allowed to swear—but not in front of visitors. In town, they will automatically be fined if they swear. He says that when they reach maturity the swearing will stop. But how can you turn a habit on and off?

"And if the idea of Summerhill is to bring up unaffected children, why shouldn't they swear and be themselves in town, too?

"Why should such importance be given to swearing anyway? As things are handled by Neill, Summerhill becomes a dark refuge where you are free to curse or speak obscenities."

At another class discussion, a student says:

"I don't know any parents who prohibit masturbation, but I know few parents who encourage it. After reading Neill I wonder if I'm supposed to tell my eleven-year-old daughter to go ahead and masturbate. Will the message create the need?"

Says another student:

> "I read this book very slowly, and I must admit truthfully that my own thinking underwent countless changes as I digested the material and experimented with it in both my personal life and in my classroom. Mr. Neill believes that the cause of all difficult people, children and adults alike, is unhappiness. They are at war with themselves; and in consequence, at war with the world.
>
> "Even though I agree with Neill's goals, I have a number of objections to Neill's belief that a child should be allowed to live out his destructive stages. That does not seem to me to be a sound principle. That principle sets a double standard for each Summerhill child: he has one code of conduct at Summerhill, and a different code of conduct when in society. I assume that is most confusing for the child, though Neill claims it is not. Even within the family structure, child experts warn that a single set of values should be agreed upon by both parents in their dealings with the child."

* * * *

I agree with my enthusiastic students on many points. Neill's approach was radical, not only in its opposition to British traditional education, but also in comparison with other progressive educational systems of that day. Whether we favor small private schools or big school systems, centralization or decentralization, community control, or student power, reading Summerhill causes us to think hard about the goals of education.

The normal child and the normal youth are eager to commit themselves to a cause which offers stimulation and direction. Such commitment enables them to belong to and to participate in a group. We learn from Adler that the "way to improvement" lies in increasing one's cooperative abilities. We also learn that mere conformity to society's accepted beliefs and timid adherence to conventional modes of thought and behavior add nothing to the spiritual wealth of the community.

Unfortunately most children fail to develop interests which would add joy and usefulness to their lives. What a child likes to do is influenced by what he has had an opportunity *to learn* to do. The richer the opportunities offered a child, the more likely that he will find those interests that best match his particular gifts.

Interests will also be influenced by the special talents the child happens to have. In all likelihood, many an adult possesses latent talents which he would now value highly if such potentialities had been cultivated when he was young.

Many of us accept Pestalozzi's dictum:

> *"Man is good and wishes to be good; but in so doing, he also wishes to be happy; if he is bad, you can be sure that someone has blocked the road on which he wished to achieve this goal."* [1]

> *"It is life that educates. All the child does, his emotional, intellectual and vocational education, must be closely connected with real life."* [2]

The concept that the child is born bad and is tainted by original

[1] Pestalozzi Johann Heinrich *How Gertrude Teaches Her Children*, first edition, 1801.
[2] Pestalozzi, Johann Heinrich, *Swan Song*, 1825.

sin is as far from the truth as Rousseau's and Neill's concept that the child is born good. Whether the child develops into a bad person or a good person depends mainly on his education.

There is almost no child born without potentialities for becoming good or becoming bad, according to the values of the society into which he is born.

The child must be enabled to learn through psychologically and socially educative trial and error. This tremendous task demands years and years of help. It is a process of learning and relearning. There is no end to the pitfalls, and mistakes, and misinterpretations. The child will be exposed to biases offered by an environment which draws inspiration from what is, in certain instances, an outdated past. In this unending interplay between the individual's potentialities and the impact of the society in which he is evolving, he as an individual and society as well are both growing, to use Allport's phrase, in an eternal "becoming."

* * *

Freud wondered whether we should ever be able to build a well-constructed society except by disregarding the individual happiness of its members. "Society," he said "repesents the authority whose punishment we fear, and for which we have submitted to so many repressions." In another place Freud says, "The price of progress in civilization is paid by forfeiting happiness."

Despite my profound respect for that great pioneer, I should like to suggest that all the concepts so heavily emphasized by Freud in *Civilization and its Discontents* simply attest to what Adler called an "erroneous style of life" and "inferiority complex." Freud conceived that man was born with two "instincts" which he saw as clear and important: Sex and Death (Eros and Thanatos).

But Freud also told us that if we wanted to survive—and he rightly saw that we could survive only as social beings—we should have to repress or sublimate these two destructive instincts. Thus he believed civilization could replace the pleasure drive of the child with a "human spirit"—a libido that had been deadened, sublimated, or made "realistic."

Although Neill accepts the Freudian concept of repression or sublimation of these socially destructive instincts, Neill does not suggest that anything should be done educationally about these instincts. Neill believes that merely by giving a child freedom, that child will live out his various stages of growing-up, and will then proceed to naturally develop to his highest potential.

Neill rightly argues:

> "Suppression awakens defiance, and defiance naturally seeks revenge. Criminality is revenge. To abolish crime, we must abolish the things that make a child want vengeance. We must show love and respect for the child."

*　*　*

In talking about the delinquent children he has handled, Neill says:

> "Make him (the child) free from inhibitions and discipline, I thought, and he will most likely turn out to be clever, creative, even brilliant. I was wrong, sadly wrong. Years of living and dealing with all sorts of delinquents have shown me that they are, for the most part, inferiors. I can think of only one boy who made his mark in later life. Quite a few were cured of being anti-social and dishonest, and they later went to work at regular jobs. But none rose to become a good

scholar or a fine artist or a skilled engineer or a talented actress. When the anti-social drive was abolished, for most of these wayward children there seemed to remain only a dead dullness that knew not ambition."

It seems to me that this had to be expected in the case of Summerhill children because they were not stimulated to new adventures of learning and living.

I followed a different tack. I believed and still believe that to discuss with the inexperienced child our own experiences, to stimulate, to challenge him to cooperative work, is to help him to a wider horizon. Such discussion becomes indoctrination *only if we make it so.* It becomes indoctrination in reverse, if we belittle the importance of learning by our indifference to education.

❋   ❋   ❋

"Punishment can never be dealt out with justice, for no man can be just. Justice implies complete understanding. Judges are no more moral than garbage collectors, nor are they less free of prejudice.

"We cannot be just because we do not know ourselves, and do not recognize our own repressed strivings. This is tragically unfair to the children. An adult can never educate beyond his own complexes. If we ourselves are bound by repressed fears, we cannot make our children free . . . Today, I know from experience that punishment is unnecessary. I never punish a child, never have any temptation to punish a child."

I agree with Neill that punishment, always an expression of the punishers urge to punish, is wrong. Punishment cannot be applied with justice. But even if we could come close to justice, I still believe punishment has no place in education. This, of course, is also true for fines in any form. To have to pay for purposely damaged goods is the consequence of breaking them. But here, too, I would never extract more than one fourth of the damages at a time from a boy's allowance or from his earnings; and I would, if the repayments were too onerous, help the child to pay for the results of his transgression.

* * *

In his book *Victory Over Myself* Floyd Patterson once Champion Heavyweight of the World, one of my former Wiltwyck boys, wrote:

> *"It was a wonderful thing when I first heard the idea explained to me by E. P., a psychoanalyst who was the executive director when I was in Wiltwyck. 'Punishment,' he said, 'teaches the child only how to punish. Scolding teaches him how to scold. By showing him that we understand, we teach him to understand. By helping him, we teach him to help. He learns cooperation by cooperating.'*
>
> *"For a boy like me, a Negro for whom there had been a growing awareness of what a difference in color meant, the interracial activities— whites being treated the same as the colored with no preference at all—this was a tremendous awakening. All religions were represented among the boys; but none was treated better or worse than any of the others."*

On the same page, Patterson says that he hated school so much, that when playing hookey he hid out in a hole in a subway tunnel where the workers kept their tools. He sat in that hole from 9 A.M. to 3 P.M., just in order to avoid getting caught on the street. There was no ventilation and no light, and the only illumination came from passing trains.

When Patterson arrived in Wiltwyck, he still wasn't interested in going to school. "They asked me to go," he writes, "but there was no punishment," implying that since he didn't care to go to class, and wasn't forced to, he simply skipped class. One day, before the kids were out of class, he met me in the courtyard and asked me about the animals he had seen in the woods. Then he asked, "Can you tell me why the leaves on the trees are small and light green in spring, big and dark green in summer, red or brown in the fall, and why there are no leaves on the trees in winter?"

"I could explain that to you," I answered, "but why don't you go to school and ask the teacher? She knows the answers too, and you can ask her whatever you want to know. Don't you want to go to school and learn something?"

His answer was annihilating. "Nobody ever told me I should go to school *to learn.* When my mother told me to go to school, she said the truant officer would come and get me if I didn't. When the truant officer came and took me, he said, 'You have to stay in school, or the court will send you to an institution. Nobody ever told me to go to school to learn what I wanted to know.'"

"The child," Edouard Claparede once wrote, "is not a child because he lacks experience; he is a child because he has the natural drive to acquire that experience." Too often we do not know how to make our children aware that school is a place to acquire interesting experiences. Education has too long been what Mark Twain once called "the organized fight of the grown-ups against youth." Our society has always claimed it was educating for the future; more often, education has been oriented to sterile conformity with the norms of the present; and all too frequently to the norms of a dead past. The good child, we thought, was one who drew from the history of mankind that the future of the race lay in unquestioning acceptance of established values. The "good" child was not told to regard the past just as a stepping-stone— although an immensely important stepping-stone no doubt—to a future which youth must create for itself. I am wholeheartedly with Neill in his opposition to this sort of education. It is up to the educators to turn Claparede's vision into a workable principle. For the child is more than willing. It is primarily up to us to make learning a wonderful experience for the young.

John Dewey suggested that education was basically a process of living, not some kind of preparation for future living. William H. Kilpatrick said that education "is life itself." Both had discovered that in education, the process and the goal are one and the same.

This process is a continuing reconstruction, wherein learning of past experiences increases interest in and desire for more and more new experiences. Learning motivates more learning. If the child is not made to fully understand the opportunities that school education offers him, we are depriving that child of his opportunities right from the beginning.

The educational program of every school has to become an integrated part of the child's life. It is necessary to incorporate as much as possible of the child's experiences into the curriculum. Learning to act reasonably in school is carried over into the home, and in turn, into a child's future life.

Learning is a process that demands interest, motivation, and guidance. It is the function and responsibility of the school to make it possible for all types of desirable learning to flower. Moreover, it is the task of the school to see that the most valuable things are learned in the most economical way, by application of the most efficient methods. But the chief goal of education is to teach the pupil *how* to learn.

*   *   *

Learning implies that a change has been produced in the learner's attitude and in his reactions. Learning involves self-control.

The development of *constructive* attitudes which will facilitate the child's life adjustment is more important than the traditional emphasis on the acquisition of specific skills and information. I agree in this with Neill. However, I would like to extend his concept of mutual understanding and respect from the equal *restriction* of freedom (where one's own freedom is limited by the freedom of others) to the whole-hearted *commitment* of each individual to the common good of our common society.

*   *   *

> *"It was really very simple. He had the ability to see everybody as they really are—just people, no more and no less. Also he saw children as people, little young people with individuality, not as some separate group of beings called children, dominated by the so-called adult world."*

I quote from Claude Brown's *Manchild in the Promised Land*:[3] The highest respect you can pay a child is to request his becoming a more responsible and cooperative human being.

Neill, referring to some of his recalcitrant charges, writes:

> *"I have seen how unhappy and hateful they are, how inferior, how emotionally confused. They*

[3] Claude Brown, *Manchild in the Promised Land*, McMillan, New York, 1965, where he describes his experience in Wiltwyck with the author.

> *are arrogant and disrespectful to me because I*
> *am a teacher, a father substitute, an enemy. I*
> *have lived with their tense hate and suspicion.*
> *But here in Summerhill, these potential delin-*
> *quents govern themselves in a self-governing*
> *community; they are free to learn and they are*
> *free to play. When they steal, they may even be*
> *rewarded. They are never preached at, never made*
> *afraid of authority, either earthly or heavenly."*

In my own experience with ten thousands of children, I have never encountered a child who was disrespectful to me because, from the very first day of our acquaintance on, I always respected him. I rarely saw a child become my enemy because I was always his friend.

Here's how Claude Brown describes his first day at Wiltwyck School:[4]

> *"After a while, Papanek stopped talking and*
> *asked if there were any questions. After the first*
> *question, it seemed that Papanek was talking with*
> *everybody, not to us. Papanek might have been a*
> *little crazy, but he meant all the crazy things he*
> *said to the boys and counselors . . . If you asked*
> *him the hard Wiltwyck questions like 'When am I*
> *going home?' . . . and Papanek couldn't tell you,*
> *he wouldn't lie about it. He would tell you some-*
> *thing that left you knowing no more than before,*
> *but you would feel kind of satisfied about it . . .*

---

[4] The author was for nine years the executive director of Wiltwyck School for Boys, a residential treatment home for severely emotionally disturbed delinquents.

And even though cats up at Wiltwyck lied a
whole lot, like me, we didn't like grown-ups to
lie to us about important things like the hard
questions."

Like Neill, wherever I worked with deviate children, I had to
live with their tense hate and suspicion. Whether they had come
to Montmorency, or to Brooklyn, or to Wiltwyck—and they were
certainly confused about what they were going to encounter when
they came—they were soon disarmed. On first sight, they began
to suspect they hadn't been loosed among enemies. For our respect was genuine. This respect included our belief that these
youths could learn and could acquire skills. We started out by
believing that each delinquent could become, not a stealing,
cursing, hating member of society, but a fully accepted and fully
contributing member of society. We did not request their obedience but their understanding. We anticipated and expected friendship because we offered them ours. We did not reward them for
stealing, because we disapproved of stealing. Nor was our friendship and love withdrawn because of their stealing. We tried to
discuss their reasons for stealing, and what help we could give
them to stay clear of larceny. This help might sometimes be in
the form of a loan, or might be a raising of allowances for all
the boys.

❋   ❋   ❋

I need not belabor the points on which I agree with Neill. I
certainly will not argue as to whether Summerhill's Saturday
meetings were better or were worse than our Thursday meetings
at Wiltwyck, or at the Brooklyn Training School for Girls, or our
Tuesday and Thursday meetings at the Montmorency Children
Homes in France. We always followed the principle of one person
one vote. But we never had court hearings or fines because we

never imposed punishment.

There were, however, "natural consequences." In France, we had a kind of children's court which held open hearings on seriously discussed cases. In all the eleven children's homes with which I have been associated with a total enrollment of approximately 1,600 children, not more than five or six sessions of these courts were held in any school over a period of two years. Judgment was arrived at, and the reasons worked out why the behavior of the accused was unacceptable to the community. Except in one case, the presentation itself was enough to make the point clear to the offender without further consequences.

The same concept was followed in the two New York homes for juvenile delinquents with which I have been associated. In these institutions, there was a therapist or a social worker or an educator who, in emotionally and psychologically difficult cases, did the analyzing, the reasoning, and the explaining.

* * *

If we want to make education the winner in the race with disaster, education must do the best job that can be done. We must enlist the best professionals available, and we must recruit young people who must themselves be properly educated for the job. These young teachers must not only be trained; we must *continue* to train them in permanent in-service training.

* * *

Neill has made radical changes in two sectors: structure and teaching. He has successfully combatted several educational archaisms, and he has replaced them with his own distinctive personality. We learn a lot from him as to what is bad in education. We do not learn enough from him as to what we can do to better the situation.

Neill was not ready to attack the social foundations—hence the psychological foundations—of his era. His approach was quite radical—some fifty years ago. Neill's message is still important, but it is no longer radical. After 50 years, I suggest some revision is due.

Goodwin Watson has had a long and distinguished career as a teacher at Columbia University, and now bears the title of Professor Emeritus of Social Psychology and Education at that institution.

He has achieved international renown as the author of a number of books among which may be mentioned: THE MEASUREMENT OF FAIR-MINDEDNESS, REDIRECTING TEACHER EDUCATION, NO ROOM AT THE BOTTOM, AUTOMATION AND THE RELUCTANT LEARNER, CHANGE IN SCHOOL SYSTEMS, *and* CONCEPTS FOR SOCIAL CHANGE. *In addition to these longer treatises, he has written several hundred articles on various aspects of education and psychology. His most recently published work is* SOCIAL PSYCHOLOGY: ISSUES AND INSIGHTS.

At present, Dr. Watson is associated with Antioch College in Yellow Springs, Ohio.

Goodwin Watson

Campuses from California to Maine and from Miami to Seattle, have feared or experienced uprisings of frustrated students. A. S. Neill's pioneer experiment at Summerhill has demonstrated what freedom (not license) can do to transform the petty tyranny of most elementary and high school classrooms. Numerous schools for young children and a few secondary schools have ventured along similar paths. Are the same basic, underlying principles applicable to the undergraduate college and to the graduate school? Would they, if incorporated in the life of an institution of higher education, alleviate the current student distress? Would the institutions then be as educative as are the best of traditional colleges?

From reading Neill's books and articles, from a visit to Summerhill, and from several other talks with him, the writer ventures to distill five principles which differentiate Neill's work from that of most other schools.

1. Learning is self-motivated rather than imposed.

Neill assumes that it is natural for children to want to learn. The evidence from the behavior of pre-school children strongly supports this view. If, as they grow older, they cease to seek new knowledge and try to escape from school requirements, this changed behavior has been brought about by the bad procedures of formal education. It took some of the pupils at Summerhill many weeks of idleness before they could recover from the distorted school-nurtured perception of learning as inherently disagreeable.

Consider the following quotations from this master-educator.

> *"The function of the child is to live his own life—not the life that his anxious parents think he should live, nor a life according to the purpose of the educator who thinks he knows what is best."* [1]

> *"Love is being on the side of the other person. Love is approval. I know that children learn slowly that freedom is something totally different from license. But they can learn this truth and do learn it."* [2]

> *"The method of freedom is almost sure with children under twelve, but children over twelve take a long time to develop from a spoon-fed education."* [3]

Douglas McGregor in his book *The Human Side of Enterprise* [4] develops an analogous principle for the management of adult workers. If the manager follows "Theory X", he believes that workers are naturally lazy: they will work only if "motivated" by the stick of fear and the carrot of advancement in pay and prestige. He assumes that unless closely supervised, his workers will goof off. So he runs a tight ship. He treats the workmen as unable or unwilling to discipline themselves or to share in planning the work to be done. He drives the crews.

If his theory of motivation be, in contrast, "Theory Y," he be-

[1] *Summerhill,* p. 12
[2] *Summerhill,* p. 293
[3] *Summerhill,* p. 293
[4] McGraw Hill, N. Y., 1960.

lieves that men enjoy devising work plans and carrying them out. He believes they can be trusted to share in decisions about what is to be done, by whom, when, and how. He believes that they will become more rather than less productive, if they are self-directing.

Now the fascinating fact is that each theory is a self-fulfilling prophecy. The employer, using Theory X, can cite abundant evidence that his workers do try to shirk, to evade, and to deceive their supervisors. If he lets up on the pressures, the men do goof off. They have no apparent interest in helping to run the business; that job they leave to the boss. He can prove the necessity of his strict controls.

But likewise, the employer who relies on Theory Y, can cite from his own experience, instances which confirm his different expectations. Given opportunity to participate in finding better ways to do the job, the workers are interested, involved, creative and practical. Sensing that they are trusted, they become increasingly responsible and self-disciplined. They often go beyond job-definitions and requirements to meet unexpected emergencies. They turn out fewer defective parts when they are their own inspectors.

The educational situation is similar. Teachers who assume that pupils will try to do as little work as they can possibly get away with, will behave in ways which make their expectations come true. The pupils will turn out to be apathetic, lazy, dependent, and in need of close direction by the teacher. The Summerhill type of teacher will have an opposite experience which confirms his predictions. Pupils given freedom to decide what they will do, when, and how, develop increasing independence, stronger interests, and better quality of work.

This is why arguments between traditional teachers and progressive facilitators are so unproductive. Each has first-hand evidence confirming his own assumptions.

There are some other truths underlying Neill's approach which also support freedom to learn rather than attempts to impose instruction. One is that what teachers think they are teaching by traditional methods does not correspond very closely to what pupils are actually learning. The teacher feels better if he has "covered the subject" (a ridiculous aspiration in this culture of accelerated explosion of knowledge) but he can easily discover that what pupils recall a week later is but a tiny fraction of what he had hoped to impart. What is learned is largely the result of the learner's own efforts. An energetic teacher may well reduce the effort which pupils feel called upon to make. So emerges the common predicament of a pupil who felt he understood the subject quite clearly while the teacher was explaining it, only to find, when tested later, that he is very confused and vague about the whole matter.

Still another truth about learning, which Summerhill took into account better than do the usual school procedures, is that there are different styles and rhythms of learning. Not all pupils in the first grade, the sixth grade or the twelfth grade, are *ready* to learn the same thing at the same time. Some were ready long before the teacher got to the new material. Others got hung up by something days earlier, or weeks or even years earlier; and until this block is removed, they are not ready to move on to whatever comes next in the teacher's syllabus.

Even among those who are ready for a given act of learning, there are still important differences. Some will grasp the whole idea in a flash; others need the slower step-by-step approach. Some will learn better from their friends than from an adult teacher. Some require first-hand encounter with experience; others can use pictures; only a few learn best from print or from being told.

Intensity of learning effort normally rises and falls. Any adult writer or scholar or thinker or artist knows that for days at a time he may be unproductive, but then suddenly he finds himself taking hold, digging in, grappling with the problems and making extraordinary progress. The formal school takes no account of this natural rhythm in learning. It assumes that each morning when the bell rings, pupils will be able to put out the standard quota of learning effort required to progress at a standard rate through the standard curriculum. Everyone concerned with schools knows that this is factually untrue, but it is maintained as an assumption to rationalize present procedures.

Let us listen again for a moment to Neill's wisdom!

> *"Let me emphasize again that a child must be left to grow at its own rate. Many parents make dreadful mistakes in trying to force the pace."* [5]

> *Q. What would you do with a child who won't stick to anything? He is interested in music for a short period, then he changes to dancing, and so on. A. I'd do nothing. Such is life. In my time I have changed from photography to bookbinding, then to woodwork, then brasswork. Life is full of fragments of interests. For many years I sketched in ink; when I realized I was a tenth-rate artist I gave it up.*

> *"A child is always eclectic in his tastes. He tries all things. That's how he learns. We never suggest that a child should finish his work; if his interest has gone, it is wrong to pressure him to finish it."* [6]

[5] *Summerhill,* p. 362
[6] *Summerhill,* p. 361

Carl R. Rogers has helped many teachers to learn the basic truth that the best learning for personal growth occurs in a non-threatening situation. A major distinction between Summerhill and all the other British boarding schools has been the absence of coercive threats in Neill's school. Because there is no need to impose and to threaten, the pupil can become more truly himself. He can learn to listen to his real feelings, and to be responsive to them. He is free to change and to grow. He does not need to use a large part of his energy to defend his autonomy or to evade those who would take freedom from him. Hence he can discover interests and concerns which lead to the kind of learning which is satisfying. There is no battle against the teacher or the curriculum. Learners and teachers become natural collaborators.

As Neill has said:

> *"True freedom practiced in community living, as in Summerhill, seems to do for the many what psychoanalysis does for the individual. It releases what is hidden. It is a breath of fresh air blowing through the soul to cleanse it of self-hatred and hatred of others."* [7]

2. *Affective learning is even more important than cognitive acquisition.*

Neill was concerned basically with the feelings of his pupils. He was central in their lives not because of his scholarship in some academic field but because of his ability to understand and to accept their actual feelings. Again and again, in his case reports, he rejects the offered mask and calls forth the true reactions hidden beneath the "proper" surface. This he learned

[7] *Summerhill*, p. 297

from psychoanalysis and his discussions with Wilhelm Reich. He concludes:

> "Knowledge in itself won't help unless a parent (or student) is emotionally ready to receive the knowledge and has the inner capacity to act on what new knowledge comes his way."[8]

> "When I lecture to students at teacher training colleges and universities I am often shocked at the ungrownupness of these lads and lasses stuffed with useless knowledge . . . They have been taught to know but have not been allowed to feel."[9]

Concern for feelings leads to greater awareness of the role of the body. The old dualism between mental and physical had no place in Neill's work. The "whole child" is now a trite expression, but it was a vital reality at Summerhill. Again, Neill found Reich congenial because Reich had pioneered insights into the way muscular tensions and other physiological changes revealed attitudes which might be verbally denied.

> "If you educate children in freedom, they will be more conscious of themselves, for freedom allows more and more of the unconscious to become conscious. That is why most Summerhill children have few doubts about life. They know what they want. And I guess they will get it, too."[10]

[8] Summerhill, p. 355
[9] Summerhill, p. 25
[10] Summerhill, p. 348

In the affective life, sex always plays a vital role. Our whole society has today moved far in the direction pioneered by Neill.

When Neill began his professional work it was in a culture which still retained the stiff standards of Puritanism and the prudery associated with Queen Victoria. As in the Vienna where Freud made his great discoveries, most neurotic behavior arose from forms of sexual repression. Immense changes have taken place during Neill's lifetime. The naughty four-letter words are commonplace in current periodicals. Nudity is no longer seen as intrinsically indecent and appears on the stage and in films.

One of Neill's important services to pupils and their parents was his early recognition of the corrupting effect of the prevailing prudishness. He shocked many by his open acceptance of normal sexual interests. This aspect of culture has changed so radically during the past generation or two, that it is hard today to realize that Neill's sensible attitude toward sex was once the basis for much hostile criticism. It seems fair to conclude that in today's freer world, Neill would have been even more outspoken. Granting all the progress that has been made, we must recognize that true sexual freedom has been attained by very few persons in our current society.

3. *The quality of living in the here and now takes precedence over efforts to prepare for the future.*

Here is perhaps the most basic contrast between the goals of Summerhill and those of schools which regard themselves as essentially "preparatory." The prep school exists to facilitate some future good. Any violation of the quality of life for pupils in the traditional school is defended on the ground that it is necessary as a preparation for entrance to the university or for securing a future job. Attendance at boring classes, reading of dull books, writing of required but distasteful papers, taking of acutely painful and humiliating tests—all these cruelties to children are rationalized as good preparation for some life to come.

This shift in values from some supposed future (viewed in a rather murky crystal ball) to the evident here-and-now was brought home to the writer when he talked one day with the mother and teacher of Harry, a seven year old child who suffered from a disease which would almost certainly lead to death within the next four or five years. What should be the "curriculum" for Harry? What requirements should he have to meet? Clearly, in his case, the right prescription was that every day should be made as satisfying as possible.

But would it really be so different for a child with normal life expectancy? Neill probably didn't study John Dewey's philosophy of education, but if he had done so, he would have met the idea that a good life today is the best possible preparation for tomorrow. Neill was more likely to have been influenced by Robert Louis Stevenson's observation that we would not compliment a hungry man who denied himself the main course of a meal so he could save all his appetite for the dessert, before he knew whether there was going to be any dessert or not.

In any case, Neill's pupils differed from those in other private schools of Britain, in that they were not as ambitious to "succeed" by current standards. They were more apt to carry away from school a quality of living which brought satisfaction in the present. More art, more music, more relaxed play, more friendly conversation!

The work of David McClelland on "Need to Achieve" has shown that the fantasies and activities of youth have a marked influence on character traits. Summerhill pupils would probably rate much higher on need for joy and need for serenity and need for affection than on need to achieve.

4. A school should be education for creativity

In a rapidly changing society the old answers are likely to be wrong answers. Neill's pupils studied the basic skills, not for their own sake, but as instruments useful in creative activity. He wrote:

> "Creators learn what they want to learn in order to have the tools that their originality and genius demand. We do not know how much creation is killed in the classroom with its emphasis on learning." [11]

Neill contrasts his view with that of the prestigious "public schools" (really private and restricted) in England.

> "The strict school carries on the tradition of keeping the child down, keeping him quiet, respectful, castrated. Moreover the school does excellent work only in treating the head of the child. It restrains his emotional life, his creative urge. It trains him to be obedient to all the dictators and bosses of life . . . The strict school demands only power—and the fearful parent is satisfied."

5. A school should be a democratic community.

At Summerhill town meetings each person—man, woman or child—director, teacher, household staff, or pupil—has one vote. Each has an equal right to attend or to stay away: to do his thing in his own way. It is not anarchy, for there are norms and rules. The rules are made by a legislative process in which the

[11] *Summerhill,* p. 26

whole community participates. Each individual wins the respect and influence which others freely give. There are no uniforms or badges of status.

> "*Summerhill is a self-governing school, democratic in form. Everything connected with social, or group life, is settled by vote at the Saturday night General School Meeting. Each member of the teaching staff and each child, regardless of his age, has one vote. My vote carries the same weight as that of a seven-year-old.*"[12]

Neill's conception of the teaching staff in any good school reflects the same quality of human relations.

> "*Teachers would be taught to be the equal of pupils, not the superiors. They would retain no protective dignity, no sarcasm. They would inspire no fear. They would have to be men and women of infinite patience, able to see far ahead, willing to trust in ultimate results.*"[13]

The principles which underlie life at Summerhill can equally well be applied at the college level. They might well revolutionize higher education. It is a strange paradox that self-directed education has been attempted most often at the nursery school and kindergarten level. As the pupil grows older and more competent, he is less and less likely to be trusted to make his own educational decisions.

Much of the student protest is directed at those aspects of

[12] *Summerhill,* p. 45
[13] *Summerhill,* p. 287

contemporary campus life which contradict the Summerhill philosophy. Students resist imposed requirements. They want to pursue kinds of learning which seem to them interesting and relevant. They are infuriated by close supervision and want to run their own lives. They want to remove the threats of tests and grades. They seek for ecstasy as well as knowledge. They want joyful experiences in the here-and-now, and they refuse to climb the ladders set up by the Establishment. They want creative living. They want to be respected as equals and not derogated to the role portrayed in an oft-quoted paper entitled "The Student as Nigger." They want power to shape decisions which have a bearing on their own lives. A short summary of what the student activists are now demanding is that they want their colleges to be more like Summerhill!

Neill may well be pleased at the student demands. He once wrote:

> *"I wish I could see a movement of rebellion among our younger teachers. Higher education and university degrees do not make a scrap of difference in confronting the evils of society."* [14]

Some of the more experimental colleges already include features which, by Neill's principles, are sound. At Antioch, Goddard, and New College (Sarasota, Florida) it is possible for a student to propose a large part of his own educational program and to carry this out in whatever way he wants to. As at Summerhill, there are courses available if a student wants to learn that way. He may, however, do independent study while living on the campus, or he may go to a Field Center in this country or abroad where he can have experiences with a style of life quite different from those he

[14] *Summerhill*, p. 28

has previously known at home or at college. He has a voice and vote in determining policies on his campus. Coeducational dormitories are accepted, and restrictive rules are few. Creativity is appreciated rather than repressed.

To extend such opportunities more widely, the Union for Research and Experimentation in Higher Education, a consortium of a dozen or more unusually progressive colleges,[15] has proposed the formation of a *University Without Walls*. Basic features have been listed as follows:

1. Admission: Persons 16-60 years of age, interested to learn.

2. Program for each student worked out individually to meet his needs and interests.

3. An Inventory of Learning Resources, well-indexed, (computer memory-bank?) will direct the learner to sources (print, tape, persons, laboratories, etc.) of knowledge he seeks.

4. Courses, laboratories, studios, etc. in all the participating colleges will be open to qualified U.W.W. students, but most of the learning will be independent and self-directed, carried out by the student alone or with a small group of peers.

5. A student begins his work by attending for one quarter (10 weeks?) a center on or near the campus of one of the participating colleges. Here he meets his fellow students, a team of faculty representing different special-

[15] Antioch, Bard, Goddard, Hofstra, Loretto Heights, Monteith, Nasson, New College at Sarasota, Northeastern Illinois State, Sarah Lawrence, Shimer, Stephens.

ties, and with his advisor works out his personal learning program. He attends two groups during the first quarter—one directed to understanding self and others (L-group); the other toward improving basic learning skills.

6. From time to time, a student will again join a group of peers (with homogeneous or heterogeneous interests) at one of the campus centers.

7. At least one term will be spent in an off-campus field center; some students may live for a time in each of several different subcultures in the U.S.A. and abroad.

8. A dialogue is continuously maintained between each student and his advisor. This may be done face-to-face, or by letters, or telephone, or tapes, or records, or papers read and returned with comments. Communication between a student and other faculty, and a student with his peers is also expected.

9. "Faculty" for the U.W.W. may include, in addition to persons teaching in one of the participating colleges, experts from any walk of life: agriculture, business, science, the arts, politics, etc.

10. Each student will complete at least one major project of excellent quality in his chosen field of work.

11. Each student keeps a cumulative record of his activities and learning. He may use standardized tests for his own guidance.

12. If a student wants a Bachelor of Arts degree he applies when he believes he is ready for it. No fixed Commencement dates. His achievements are reviewed by a committee of faculty and students, who recommend a degree or further study.

The name—*University Without Walls*—recalls Neill's statement about most school buildings:

> *"The classroom walls and prison-like buildings narrow the teacher's outlook and prevent him from seeing the true essentials of education."* [16]

The Summerhillian principles suggest also a need for fundamental change in post-graduate education. In most universities today, Ph.D. programs are discipline-oriented with prescribed course requirements, certification examinations within the subject area, and research of a fairly standard pattern. Yet the needs of students and of society would require a more flexible program which is person-oriented and problem-focused. Again the U.R.E.H.E. has come forward with a proposal.

The proposed Graduate School of U.R.E.H.E. will provide opportunity for capable students to go beyond the B.A. to a Ph.D. The design continues many features of the University Without Walls. Programs are designed to fit the needs of each individual student. Interdisciplinary work is encouraged. Any course in any

[16] *Summerhill*, p. 28

university in the world may be included. Dialogue between student and a faculty committee is maintained. Students review their progress, from time to time, in a colloquium of fellow-candidates. Each student keeps a cumulative record of his progress. His graduate work culminates in a major project which may be research, or a book, or a work of art, or an achievement in social change, or may take other forms. The doctorate may be applied for, and on recommendation of faculty and peers, awarded at any time. The program will begin at several different geographic centers in 1970.

Summerhill was the creation of an earlier era, related to a different world from that in which we today struggle for survival. Without negating the valid view of personal development and the learning process which Neill developed, we are pressed to take more account of unsolved social problems. In the United States, extrication from the Viet Nam war and the prevention of similar allegedly anti-Communist military escapades in future years is of primary concern. So is the continuing battle against poverty and against white racism. Environmental pollution is another center of concern. The right of women and children to be fully respected as persons and not chattels has yet to be fully realized.

The specific grievances are contemporary but the basic concern that schools should make a difference in society was apparent in Neill's philosophy. He saw, as noted above, a clear connection between authoritarian control in the classroom and submission to dictatorship in the nation.

In another passage—anticipating the central thesis of Norman O. Brown's *Life Against Death*[17]—Neill wrote about society as well as school:

"Pro-life equals fun, games, love, interesting

[17] Life Against Death, Homan O. Brown; New York, Vintage Books

work, hobbies, laughter, music, dance, considera-
tion for others, and faith in men. Anti-life equals
duty, obedience, profit and power. Throughout
history anti-life has won, and will continue to win
as long as youth is trained to fit into present-day
adult conceptions." [18]

At a recent conference of innovative college faculty members
and students (New College, Sarasota, Florida, June 30-July 12,
1969) the following statements were adopted almost unanimously
and have been central to student protests in many colleges.

> *"This culture is oppressive.*
>
> *"There is no human task more important than*
> *creating alternatives to our culture.*
>
> *"Alternatives begin in self-liberation.*
>
> *"A lack of trust infects American society and*
> *we cannot survive without trust.*
>
> *"Our present structures and institutions are*
> *inept—frequently accelerate the malignancy in*
> *our society, rarely do anything to arrest it and*
> *are absolutely unable to cure it and prevent*
> *further recurrences.*
>
> *"Urgent and critical problems threatening the*
> *survival of life on this violent planet demand im-*
> *mediate attention."*

These truths, if indeed they are valid, call for changes in education at every age level, from youngest children through to the

[18] *Summerhill,* p. 344

elderly and retired adults. They call for a progressive advance which incorporates the wisdom of Neill of Summerhill, but which moves further to cope with the problems emerging in America and the world on the verge of the 21st Century.

Neill himself has provided a fitting close to this proposal for a Summerhill University.

> *"The future of Summerhill itself may be of little import. But the future of the Summerhill idea is of the greatest importance to humanity. New generations must be given the chance to grow in freedom. The bestowal of freedom is the bestowal of love. And only love can save the world."*[19]

---

[19] *Summerhill,* p. 92

Sylvia Ashton-Warner, writer and school teacher, was born in Stratford, New Zealand. For 17 years, she worked in Maori schools, and her poetic style and vision reflect the very special atmosphere of her country. The publication of her book, SPINSTER, *made her world famous. In her book,* TEACHER, *published in 1963, she forges a unique approach to the problem of teaching reading.*

Her other works include GREENSTONE, BELL CALL, *and* INCENSE TO IDOLS.

Sylvia
Ashton-Warner

Dear Mr. Neill: This stiff use of the *Mister* may suggest a stiff Aunt Mary of a generation unpopular at Summerhill, a generation of children forced to learn to read, made to go to bed, and brought up to respect their elders and betters. If so, it suggests quite rightly, for I am all of that: a tough old-timer redolent of discipline. Yet even were I a young new-timer untouched by the rod, I think I'd still recognize my elders and betters and be relieved to feel respect. So I'll keep to the proper *Mister*. . . . "Hi, Neill!" would not come well from me.

This is not to mean that I agree with all you say because, as it happens, I disagree with much. But this good space can't be squandered on pedestrian disagreement.

"Books," you say in *Summerhill*, "are the least important apparatus in a school." All that any child needs, you claim, are the three R's; the rest should be tools and clay and sports and theatre and paint and any amount of freedom.

Moreover, you continue, "Parents are slow to realize how unimportant the learning side of school is. Only pedants claim that learning from books is education."

Along with all this, Mr. Neill, you tell of many a child who couldn't read or wouldn't read—some for the whole of their time at Summerhill. You tell of a boy called Jim, a poor wee chap who had been boarded out, and who compensated for his inferiority by fantasying. Ever since he arrived at Summerhill, he'd been impressing the boys. He'd talk of a rich uncle who owned two ocean liners. Jim had convinced a few of the boys of the truth of his story. They then persuaded Jim to write to this uncle and ask that tycoon for a motorboat. With the result that for days after, you saw these deluded youngsters watching the harbor approaches, waiting for a liner that would come towing their motorboat.

Another rich uncle, according to Jim, was giving him a Rolls Royce—boy's size, of course, but gasoline-driven. Fortuitously, Jim didn't need a license to drive that car; and his uncle, according to Jim, was railing the car to the local station for Jim's benefit. When you, Mr. Neill, came upon the little group heading for the railway station some four miles away, you mercifully stopped the lads, and Jim was visibly relieved.

How can a boy, you ask, be interested in mathematics—or for that matter, reading—when he is expecting a Rolls Royce? To ask him to read at such a time would be a crime, you say. Jim lived in a world of fantasy. To say to him sternly, "Put all this nonsense out of your head about uncles and motorcars. It's all made up, and you know it. You take a reading lesson tomorrow, or I'll know the reason why!"—that would be breaking that boy's world before he had something with which to replace it.

Only where a fantasy has persisted for years does one dare to break it, you continue. It took me maybe a year or so, you say, to break Jim's dream in two. And the way you did it was to encourage him to talk about his fantasy. In nine cases out of ten, a lad will slowly lose interest in his dream world. But until he has lived out his fantasies, he cannot possibly have any interest in reading. That, Mr. Neill, is your stance.

Where you say, Mr. Neill, that the best way was to encourage Jim to talk about his fantasy—that was the place where you came within a footlength of solving your reading problems. But when you maintain that to read during that time of his life would have been a crime, that is the precise place where I would have started to weld something of mine to something of yours: my *Key Vocabulary* to your freedoms.

Like all children, Jim had a mind full of vivid imagery—happy imagery of a motorcar, an uncle, an ocean liner, and a motorboat. Jim was a boy with what you call "a mechanical bent," as most boys of that age are. But there also were deeper unhappy images in Jim's mind which arose from his boarded out life which drove him to fantasy in the first place.

No one could have known what the word-symbols, the captions of Jim's mind, would be until Jim himself had revealed them, but these symbols would assuredly have represented the sorrows of his life. Maybe he was hungry; most certainly he was lonely; possibly someone had struck him. And of course, there would have been jealously of some other child who *really* belonged to a family. You see, I too, had been boarded out for a time when I was young, and I remember so well that fright was the big thing.

But what you saw in Jim as a flight fantasy to be corrected, I see as riches to have been capitalized on and harnessed. The more powerful the imagery, the more productive that imagery because such fantasy fuels feeling. Far from "breaking the dream" as you skilfully did, why not use what was there?

You might have begun by engaging Jim in relevant conversation. Soon the key words would have surfaced: his desires, his fears, his feelings, his ideas, and his dangerous instincts—the thoughts that were the key to his mind: the *Key Vocabulary*.

The first words would likely have been the happy captions of his obsession: *Rolls Royce, ocean liner, motorboat, uncle,* and many others related to these. After which would have come the symbols of his former pain, the source of the infection. Why could you not have used these very words for his first reading lesson?

You say, how can a boy have an interest in reading when he's expecting a Rolls Royce? He can if his reading is *about* Rolls Royce. How can alien words possibly enter a mind already crammed to bulging point with excited imagery? How can one push in any door when there's no standing-room in the chamber? But the words to have taught Jim would not have been alien words imposed from outside, but words and concepts already inside him.

It is alright to ask a child with a normal mind to learn to read; his house is not too full to find room for strangers; he can take reading in his stride. But Jim could have learned to read the words which already were his own—words which represented vital thoughts yearning to take on form. If you had written these captions on big easy cards telling Jim what they were, if you had guided his fingers around the shapes of the big easy letters, naming these letters, too; and if you had then asked Jim what the words were, he'd have known them alright. He'd not have to be taught a second time.

He would have learned more than the words themselves; he'd have learned that a written word could be of intense personal importance to him: captions of his Rolls Royce and his ocean liner. He would have even agreed to write these words given the means: either a large piece of paper and a sturdy crayon, or a blackboard and a piece of chalk, or a sharp stick and a cleared piece of ground, or a shell on the sand, or anything else with which he could have delineated those strange marks that to his mind would have connoted . . . pictures vivid to his inner eye. He would have written those words compulsively. The only discipline would have been his own: he would have read those words and he would have written them *because he wanted to.*

Any number of key words would now slip out once the door had been opened. Maybe *license*, I don't know, but less of the captions of that place where Jim had been boarded out. And if there was a word he could not have learned, that would have been your failing—not his.

Soon Jim would have been ready to combine two words: *rich*

uncle, new car, my motorboat. Then three: *I can drive,* or perhaps, *I was hungry.* In time, Jim would have gone on to four: *My uncle is rich; I've got a Rolls Royce.* Those words would have been supplied by Jim himself, always reading with other girls and boys, sitting together reading each other's work, talking and touching each other.

With the detumescence of the mind and the gradual departure of the people crowding Jim's house, more accommodation would have in time been available for casual visitors in the form of outside words and ideas. It would no longer have been a crime to ask Jim to read. For having made friends with the written word, any time now, you might have seen Jim pick up standard books lying around. He would have become, at this time, a boy who *liked* reading . . . an altogether different thing from a boy who merely could read.

A boy with a book is much less lively at bedtime. In fact, with the help of what you term "the least important apparatus in a school", there'd be a good bit less noise around at bedtime.

Jack, you relate, was another boy who could not learn to read. Even when he asked for a reading lesson there was some hidden obstruction that kept him from distinguishing between *b* and *d*, and *g* and *p*.

I think—but I'm not sure—that you could have neutralized this obstruction had not you yourself shown a resistance to reading. If a child borrows a book, you observe, and he leaves it out in the rain, "my wife gets angry because books mean much to her." In such a case, you say, "I am personally indifferent, for books have little value for me." On the other hand, you go on, "my wife seems vaguely surprised when I make a fuss about a ruined chisel; for I value tools, while tools mean little to her."

Can it be, Mr. Neill, that tools are the most important apparatus in a school? Anyway, here we have it in your own words: *Books have little value for me.* Why?

On another page you write: "I met a girl of fourteen in Copenhagen who spent three free years in Summerhill, and had spoken perfect English."

"I suppose you are at the top of your class in English," I said. "No," she replied, "I'm at the bottom of my class because I don't know English grammar."

Why not? I wonder. Many of us delight in grammar, Mr. Neill, as much as you delight in your tools and your engineering workshop.

We have found, you remark with puzzled interest, that the boy who cannot or will not read until he is, say fifteen, is always a boy with a mechanical-bent who later becomes a good engineer or electrician. I cannot help sensing a vague relationship here between these mechanical-bent boys who will not read—Jim was one, too—and you who were also a mechanical-bent boy for whom now "books have little value."

Anyway, back to Jack, a boy who left school at seventeen still unable to read and who now you report is an expert toolmaker. Jack's own *Key Vocabulary* at five would have shown—and I don't say might have shown but would have shown twelve years in advance—that he'd go the mechanical way. Boys like Jack disgorge vocabularies pungently odorous of oil, grease, fumes, and noise: words like *truck, racing car, jet, wheels,* or more picturesquely *ocean liner, motorboat,* and *Rolls Royce.* Anything with mobility. Yet only after Jack left Summerhill did this vocabulary of his crash through under its own power. Which at the least indicates that an early *Key Vocabulary* would have liquidated the obstruction in the first place. For Jack was a boy who knew freedom. With that extra footlength of the *Key Vocabulary,* he would have been reading as soon as he handled his first tool.

Tom came to Summerhill at the age of five and left at seventeen

—I simply love this story—without having in all those years attended a single lesson. He spent much time in the workshop making things. Yet, one night when he was nine, you found him in bed reading *David Copperfield*. He had taught himself to read.

But only because the freedom you provided, as well as the opportunity for expression, had allowed Tom to approach to within one step of the *Key Vocabulary* where his imagery finally demanded words. A lovely story. Yet he could have been reading four years earlier.

Then here's another Jack who failed his university exams, you say, because he hated book learning.

Why? I wonder.

But, you add, he turned out in the end to be a successful engineer. I've heard this before, Mr. Neill. Are you a disappointed engineer?

A parent said to you one apprehensive day, "If my son cannot read at twelve, what chance has he of success in life? If he cannot pass college examinations at eighteen, what is there for him but an unskilled job?"

You answered, "I would rather see this school produce a happy street cleaner than a neurotic scholar."

Humph! so you call a street cleaner a success in life!

I like the part where you were on a collision course with Aunt Mary. "Eleven years old," she blew up, referring to her charge, "and she can't read properly!" I would have said the same myself.

For reading in itself has its own quality of healing, a certain pacifying power when one *likes* reading. The important thing is that one should not only learn to read but should *desire* to read. Once a child desires to read, learning itself combusts.

Through your philosophy, Mr. Neill, run veins of Zen Buddhism. Suzuki himself could have said:

> *I believe in the child as a good, not an evil being.*
>
> *The function of the child is to live his own life —not the life his anxious parents think he should live, not a life according to the purpose of the educator.*
>
> *The absence of fear is the finest thing for a child.*

Summerhill is good news. This Neill-Zen spirit of freedom actually authorizing happiness is very good news.

It is communication between kind that vitalizes your General School Meetings in which the children are disciplining themselves for raiding the pantry, or penalizing a bully, or debating contentiously the pros and cons of playing football in the lounge, or working out a plan for getting children to bed. (How often along your pages the age-old problem of bedtime blows up. If anything were needed to prove your sincerity, it would be your endurance at bedtime, the only answer to which I've ever had is an endless supply of books.)

You say that one weekly General School Meeting is of more value than a week's curriculum of school subjects, that the meetings are an excellent theatre for practicing public speaking, that most of the children speak well and without self-consciousness, and that you have often heard sensible speeches from children who could neither read nor write. With or without approval of each other—mostly *without* I'd say—children have more intuitive knowledge of each other than the most accomplished teacher.

I, too, can record that I have often heard electric poetry from children too young to read or write.

Paul Goodman is widely recognized as one of today's most incisive critics of society. Perhaps more than any other single person, Mr. Goodman is responsible for influencing the thinking of today's students. A prolific writer, he has been published in just about every important journal of opinion and is the author of over twenty volumes, which include GROWING UP ABSURD, LIKE A CONQUERED PROVINCE, *and* COMPULSORY MIS-EDUCATION.

A native New Yorker, he graduated from City College and was granted his doctorate by the University of Chicago. He has taught in seven universities and has lectured extensively throughout the country.

Paul Goodman

In every society, the education of the children is of the first importance. But in all societies, both primitive and highly civilized, until quite recently most education occurred incidentally. Adults did their work and other social tasks. The children were not excluded. The children were paid attention to and learned to be included; they were not "taught."

In most institutions and in most societies *Incidental Education* has been taken for granted. Incidental education takes place in community labor, master-apprentice arrangements, games, plays, sexual initiations, and religious rites.

Generally speaking, this incidental process suits the nature of learning better than direct teaching. The young experience cause and effect rather than pedagogic exercise. Reality is often complex, but every young person can take that reality in his own way, at his own time, according to his own interests and own initiative. Most importantly, he can imitate, identify, be approved, be disapproved, cooperate, or compete without suffering anxiety through being the center of attention.

The archetype of successful incidental education is that of an infant learning to speak, a formidable intellectual achievement that is universally accomplished. We do not know how it is done, but the main conditions seem to be what we have been describing: Activity is going on involving speaking. The infant participates; he is attended to and spoken to; he plays freely with his speech sounds; it is advantageous to him to make himself understood.

Along with incidental education, most societies also maintain institutions specifically devoted to teaching the young, such as identity rites, catechisms, nurses, pedagogues, youth houses, and formal schooling. I think there is a peculiar aspect to what is learned through such means, rather than what is picked up incidentally.

Let me emphasize that it is only in the last century that a majority of the children in industrialized countries have gotten much direct teaching. Only in the past few decades has formal schooling been generally extended into adolescence and further. For example, in the United States in 1900, only six percent of the youngsters went through high school, and only one quarter of one percent went through college. Yet now, formal schooling has taken over, well or badly, very much of the more natural incidental education of most other institutions.

This state of affairs may or may not be necessary, but it has had consequences. These institutions, and the adults who run them, have correspondingly lost touch with the young; and on the other hand, the young do not know the adults who are involved in their chief activities.

Like jails and insane asylums, schools isolate society from its problems, whether in preventing crime, or in curing mental disease, or in bringing up the young. To a remarkable degree, the vital functions of growing up have become hermetically redefined in school terms. Community service means doing homework. Apprenticeship means passing tests for a job in the distant future. Sexual initiation is high school dating. Rites of passage consist in getting a diploma. Crime is breaking the school windows. Rebellion is sitting in on the Dean. In the absence of adult culture, the youth develop a sub-culture.

Usually, there has been a rough distinction between the content of what is learned in incidental education and what is learned in direct pedagogy. Teaching, whether directed by elders, priests, or academics, deals with what is not evident in ordinary affairs; pedagogy aims to teach what is abstract, intangible, or mysterious.

As the center of attention, the learner is under pressure. All education socializes, but pedagogy socializes deliberately, instilling the morals and habits which are the social bonds.

There are two opposite interpretations of why pedagogy seeks to indoctrinate. In my opinion, both interpretations are correct. On the one hand, the elders instill an ideology which will support their system of exploitation and the domination of the old over the young, and they, the elders, make a special effort to confuse and mystify because their system does not recommend itself to common sense.

On the other hand, there is vague but important wisdom that must be passed on, a wisdom which does not appear on the surface and which requires special pointing out and cloistered reflection. The champions of the liberal arts colleges maintain that, one way or another, the young will pick up contemporary know-how and mores, but that the greatness of Mankind—Hippocrates, Beethoven, Enlightenment, Civil Liberties, the Sense of the Tragic—all will lapse without a trace unless scholars work at perpetuating these values. I sympathize with the problem as they state it; but, in fact, I have not heard of any method whatever, scholastic or otherwise, of teaching the humanities without killing them. I remember how at age twelve, browsing in the library, I read *Macbeth* with excitement; yet in class I could not understand a word of *Julius Caesar*, and I hated it. I'm pretty sure this is a common pattern. The survival of the humanities would seem to depend on random miracles which are becoming less frequent.

Unlike incidental learning which is natural and inevitable, formal schooling is deliberate intervention and must justify itself. We must ask not only whether such schooling is well done, but is it *worth* doing? *Can* it be well done? Is teaching possible at all?

There is a line of critics from Lao-tse and Socrates to Carl Rogers who assert that there is no such thing as teaching either science or virtue; and there is strong evidence that schooling has had little effect on either vocational ability or on citizenship. Donald Hoyt, in *American College Testing Reports* (1965) found that in any profession, college grades have had no correlation with life achievement.

At the other extreme, Dr. Skinner and the operant-conditioners claim that they can "instruct" for every kind of performance, and that they can control and shape human behavior much as they can the behavior of animals who have been sealed off from their ordinary environment. But it is disputable whether children are good subjects for such instruction in any society we might envisage.

The main line of educators from Confucius and Aristotle to John Dewey hold that one can teach the child good habits in morals, arts, and sciences through practice. The art is to provide the right tacks at the right moments; and Froebel, Herbert, Steiner, Piaget, etc., have different theories about this. But sociologists like Comte and Marx hold that social institutions overwhelmingly determine what is learned—so much so, that it is not worthwhile to be concerned with pedagogy. My bias is that "teaching" is largely a delusion.

In every advanced country, the school system has taken over a vast part of the educational functions of society. The educationists design toys for age two, train for every occupation, train for citizenship, train for sexuality, and explain and promote the humanities.

With trivial exceptions, what we mean by *school*—curriculum, texts, lessons, scheduled periods marked by bells, teachers, examinations, and graded promotion to the next step—was the invention of some Irish monks of the seventh century who thought to bring a bit of Rome to wild shepherds. It has been an amazing success story, probably more important than the Industrial Revolution.

No doubt it was a good thing, at first, for wild shepherds to have to sit still for a couple of hours and pay strict attention to penmanship and spelling. The imposed curriculum was entirely exotic and could only be learned by rote anyway. Mostly, of course, it was only aspiring clerics who were schooled.

By an historical accident, the same academic method later became the way of teaching the bookish part of some of the learned professions. There is no essential reason why law and medicine are not better learned through apprenticeship, but the bookish method was clerical, and therefore scholastic. Perhaps any special education based on abstract principles was part of a system of mysteries, and therefore clerical, and therefore scholastic.

The monkish rule of scheduled hours, texts, and lessons is also not an implausible method for giving a quick briefing to large numbers of students, who then embark on their real business. Jefferson insisted on universal compulsory schooling for short terms in predominantly rural communities, in order that children might be able to read the newspapers and be catechized in libertarian political history. During the following century, in compulsory urban schools, the children of immigrants were socialized and taught standard English. The curriculum was the penmanship, the spelling, and the arithmetic needed for the business world.

At present, however, the context of schooling is quite different. The old monkish invention of formal schooling is now used as universal social engineering. Society is conceived as a controlled system of personnel and transactions, with various national goals depending on the particular nation. And the schools are the teaching machines for all personnel.

There is no other way of entry for the young. Teaching aims at psychological preparation in depth. Schooling for one's role, in graded steps, takes up to 20 years and more; it is the chief activity of growing up; any other interest may be interrupted—but not schooling. The motivation for a five-year-old's behavior is thus geared 15 years in the future.

In highly productive technologies like ours which do not need manpower, the function of long schooling is to keep the useless and obstreperous young *away* from the delicate social machine. The function of the school is to baby-sit the young and police them.

Yet the schools are not good playgrounds or reservations either. The texture of school experience is similar to adult experience. There is little break between playing with educational toys and watching educational TV, or between being in high school and dating, or between being in college and being drafted, or between being personnel of a corporation and watching NBC.

Since the trend has been to eliminate incidental education and deliberately to prepare the young for every aspect of ordinary life through schooling, we would expect pedagogy to have become functional. Yet radical students complain that today's schooling is ideological through and through. The simplest, and not altogether superficial, explanation of this paradox is that scholastic mystery has transformed adult business. It is society that has become mandarin.

None of this works. Contemporary schooling does not prepare for jobs and professions. For example, evidence compiled by Ivar Berg of Columbia shows that, on the job, dropouts do as well as high school graduates.

Nor has today's education made for peaceful baby-sitting and policing. Instead of an efficient gearing between the teaching machine and the rest of the social machine, the schools seem to run for their own sake. There is a generation gap. Many youngsters fail; many drop out; others picket.

Predictably, the response of school administrators has been to refine the process; to make the curriculum more relevant, to start

schooling earlier, to employ new technologies in teaching, to eliminate friction by admitting students to administrative functions.

But the chief objection to engineering in education is that it is
inefficient. It tries to program too much, to pre-structure syllabi
and lesson-plans. But human behavior is strong, graceful, and
discriminating only to the extent that, in concrete situations, it
creates its own structures as it goes along. Things can be learned
securely, quickly, and naturally only through coping. As John Holt
has pointed out, the teacher wants the child to learn the lesson
according to the teaching plan; but the child quickly learns how
to con the teacher, for getting a passing grade is the child's *real*
problem of the moment.

It has frequently been said that human beings use only a small
part—"just two percent"—of their abilities. Some educators therefore propose that much more demanding and intellectual tasks be
set at a much earlier age. There is no doubt that most children
can think and learn far more than they are challenged to. Yet it
is likely that by far the greatest waste of ability occurs because
a playful, hunting, sexy, dreamy, combative, passionate, artistic,
manipulative, destructive, jealous, magnanimous, selfish and dis-
interested animal is continually thwarted by social organization—
and perhaps especially by schooling.

If so, the main purpose of pedagogy should be to counteract
and delay socialization as long as possible. For our situation is the
opposite of the situation in the seventh century. Since the world
has become overly scholastic, we must protect the wild shepherds.

Current high thought among schoolmen, for instance those of
the National Science Foundation and those of the Harvard School
of Education, is that the contemporary syllabus is indeed wasteful
and depressing. But they would expand the schools and render
the programming more psychological. Since the frontiers of knowledge are changing so rapidly, there is no use in burdening children

with data that will be outdated in ten years, or with skills that will soon be better performed by machines; rather children must learn *to learn*: their cognitive faculties must be developed; they must be taught the big Ideas, concepts like the conservation of energy. This is exactly what Robert Hutchins was saying 40 years ago.

Or more daringly, the children must not be *taught*, but be allowed to *discover*. They must be encouraged to guess and to brainstorm rather than be tested on the right answers.

In my opinion, in an academic setting, these proposals are never bona fide. As Gregory Bateson has noted with dolphins and trainers, and as John Holt has noticed in middle class schools, learning to learn means picking up the structure of behavior of the teachers, becoming expert in the academic process. In actual practice, the young discoverers are bound to discover what will get them past the College Board examinations. Guessers and dreamers are not free to balk and drop out for a semester to brood and let their theories germinate in the dark, as proper geniuses do.

It is a crucial question whether "cognitive faculties" does not mean the syntax of school performance. There is an eccentric passage in an early work of Piaget where he says that children in the playground seem to be using intellectual concepts, e.g. causality, a couple of years earlier than they are "developed" in the classroom, but he sticks to the classroom situation because it allows for his "scientific" observation. Yet this might mean that the formal routine of the classroom has hindered the spontaneous use of the intellect, and that the "concept" which is developed in the classroom is not an act of intellect grasping the world at all, but is a method of adjustment to the classroom, the constricted seats, the schedule, the teacher's expectation, the boring subject-matter to which one must pay attention.

       ✹   ✹   ✹

Progressive education is best defined as a series of reactions to a school system that has become rigid. Progressive education aims to include what has been repressed; it aims to right the balance.

Moreover progressive education is a political movement; Progressive education emerges when the social problem is breaking out. To put it more positively, an old regime is not adequate to cope with new conditions; new energy is needed. The form that progressive education takes in each era is prophetic of the next social revolution.

Rousseau reacted to the artificiality and insincerity of the royal court, and the parasitism, the callous formalism, and the pervasive superstitution of the courtiers. The establishment of his day had simply become incompetent to govern. A generation later, it abdicated.

John Dewey reacted to a genteel culture that was irrelevant in an industrialized society. Dewey reacted to rococo decoration, to puritanism that denied animal nature, to censorship, and to rote performance imposed on children. Again, after a generation, (by the end of the New Deal) Dewey's moral vision had largely come to be. In his life-time, most of the program of the Populists and the Labor movement had become law; education and culture (among whites) had become utilitarian and fairly classless; the revolution of Freud and Spock was well advanced; censorship was on its way out; and there was no more appliqué decoration.

A. S. Neill's Summerhill School, a recent form of progressive education, was likewise a reaction against social-engineering. Neill reacted against the trend to 1984 as Orwell came to call it, against obedience, authoritarian rules, organizational role-playing instead of being, the destruction wrought by competition and grade-getting. Since going to class is for children in the immutable nature of things, Neill's making of attendance a matter of choice was a transformation of reality; and to the extent that there was authentic self-government at Summerhill and to the extent that small children were indeed given power, the charisma of all institutions was challenged.

Progressive education has been criticized as a middle-class gimmick. The black community, especially, resents being used for "experiments." Poor children, it is claimed, need to learn the conventional wisdom so they can compete for power in the established system. Black parents demand "equality education" and expect their children to wear ties.

In my opinion, this criticism is wrongheaded. The scholastic evidence, shows that the more experimental the high school, the more successfully its graduates compete in conventional colleges.

Black communities should run their own schools, and they should run them on the model of Summerhill. This has indeed been the case with the sporadic Freedom Schools which have been influenced, directly or indirectly, by Neill.

I don't agree with the theory of *Head Start* that disadvantaged children require special training to prepare them for learning. I find nothing wrong with the development of their intellectual faculties; they have learned to speak, and they can make practical syllogisms very nicely, if they need to. If they have not learned the patterns by which they can succeed in school, the plausible move is to change the school. But, as Elliott Shapiro has suggested, the trouble might be that these children have been pushed too early to take responsibility for themselves and for their little brothers and sisters as well. The trouble is that their real problems have been all too insoluble. It's not that these children can't reason; the fact is that pure reason is of no use to them in their coping with their all too real difficulties.

What these kids need is freedom from pressure to perform. And, of course, they need better food, more quiet, and a less impoverished environment to grow up in—AT THEIR OWN PACE. These things are what the First Street School on the Lower East Side in New York, which was somewhat modeled on Summerhill, tried to provide.

Nevertheless, we must say that progressive education has been almost a total failure. The societies that have emerged after fulfilling their programs, were not what the visionaries had hoped for. French or American democracy was not what Rousseau had in mind. Dewey's social conceptions have ended up as technocracy, labor bureaucracy, and suburban conformity. The likelihood is that A. S. Neill's hope, too, will be badly realized. It is not hard to envisage a society in the near future in which self-reliant and happy people will be attendants of a technological infrastructure over which they have no control whatever, and whose purposes do not seem to them to be any of their business. Indeed, Neill describes with near satisfaction such success-stories among his own graduates. Alternately, it is conceivable that an affluent society will support its hippies like Indians on a reservation.

How to prevent these outcomes? Perhaps Neill protects his community a few years too long, both from the oppressive mechanistic world and from adolescent solitude—it is hard to be alone in Summerhill. Moreover, it seems to me that there is something inauthentic in Neill's latitudinarian lack of standards. For example, Beethoven and Rock 'n Roll are considered equivalent (though Neill himself prefers Beethoven). We are not only free organisms but parts of a mankind that historically has made strides with great inspirations and through terrible conflicts. We cannot slough off that accumulation of cultures, however burdensome, without becoming trivial. It seems clear to me that the noisy youth subculture of today is not grown-up—which is to the good—but also that it can *never* become grown-up.

Generally, the young of today have strong feelings for honesty, frankness, loyalty, fairness, affection, freedom and the other virtues of generous natures. They quickly resent the hypocrisy of politicians, administrators, and parents who mouth big abstractions, but who act badly. But the young themselves—like most politicians and administrators and many parents—seem to have forgotten the concrete reality of ideals like magnanimity, compassion, honor, consistency, civil liberty, integrity and justice—ideals which maintain and which re-create Mankind. Naturally, without these ideals and the conflicts they engender, there is no tragedy. Most young persons seem to disbelieve that tragedy exists, they always interpret impasse as timidity, and casuistry as finking out. I may be harsh, but though I am often astonished by their physical courage, I am not often impressed by their moral courage.

*   *   *

My own thinking is that:

(1) Incidental education (taking part in the on-going activities of society) should be the chief means of learning.

(2) Most high schools should be eliminated. Other kinds of youth communities should take over the social functions of the high school.

(3) College training, generally, should follow—not precede—entry into the professions.

(4) The chief task of educators should be to see that the activities of society provide incidental education. If necessary, government and society should invent new useful activities offering new educational opportunities.

(5) The purpose of elementary pedagogy through age twelve should be to protect and nourish a child's free growth, since both the community and family pressure are too much for a child to withstand.

Let me review the arguments for this program:

We must drastically cut back schooling because our extended tutelage is against nature and actually arrests growth.

The effort to channel growing up according to a preconceived curriculum discourages the young and wastes many of the best of our powers to learn and cope.

Schooling does not prepare for real performance; it is largely carried on for its own sake. Only the academically talented, only 10 to 15% according to Conant, thrive in this useless activity without being bored, and without being harmed.

Our system of education, isolating as it does the young from the older generation, alienates the young.

Yet it makes no sense for many of the brightest and most sensitive of our young to simply drop out or to confront society with hostility. This state of affairs does not lead to social reconstruction. The complicated and confusing conditions of our times require fresh thinking, and therefore, what we need is participation, particularly by the young.

Young radicals seem to believe that political change will solve our chief problem. Or that our problems will solve themselves after political change. This is a delusion. Our novel problems of urbanization, technology, and ecology have not heretofore been faced by any political faith. The fact is that the educational systems of other advanced countries are no better than ours.

It has been my Calvinistic and Aristotelian experience that most people cannot organize their lives without productive activity. Of course, this does not necessarily mean paid activity. The professions, the services, industries, arts and sciences are the arena. Radical politics and doing one's thing are careers for only a very few.

As things are, American society either excludes the young, or corrupts the young, or exploits the young. I believe we must make the rules of licensing and hiring more realistic, and we must get rid of mandarin requirements. We must design apprenticeships that are not exploitative.

Society desperately needs much work, both intellectual and manual, in urban renewal, in ecology, in communications, and in the arts. All these spheres could make use of young people. Many such enterprises are best organized by young people themselves, like the community development and the community action of "Vocations for Social Change." There are also excellent apprenticeships open for the brainy at think-tanks like the Oceanic Institute at Makapuu Point, or in the Institute for Policy Studies in Washington, both of which are careless about checking diplomas. Our aim should be to multiply the paths of growing up. There should be ample opportunity for a young boy or girl to begin his career again, to cross over from one career to another, to take a moratorium, to travel, or to work on his own. To insure freedom of option, and to insure that the young can maintain and express their critical attitude, adolescents should be guaranteed a living. Giving a young person the present cost of a high school education would provide enough money for a young person to live on.

The advantage of making education less academic has, of course, occurred to many school people. There are a myriad of programs to open the school to the world by: (1) recruiting professionals, artists, gurus, mothers, and dropouts as teachers' aides; and (2) granting academic credit for work-study, for community action, for the writing of novels, for service in mental hospitals, for spending one's junior year abroad, and for other kinds of released time.

Naturally, I am enthusiastic for this development, and I only want it to go the small further step of abolishing the present school establishment, instead of aggrandizing it.

There is also a movement in the United States, as there is in Cuba and China, for adolescent years to be devoted to public service. This is fine if the service is not compulsory nor regimenting.

It *is* possible for everyone's education to be tailor-made according to his own particular developing interest. Choices along the way will often be ill-conceived and wasteful, but such choices will nevertheless express desire, and will therefore immediately coincide with reality. Such choices will, therefore, converge to find the right vocation for a young person more quickly than through any other method. One's vocation is what one is good at and can do. Vocation is what employs a reasonable amount of one's powers. The use of the full power of a majority of the people would make for a stable society which would be far more efficient than our own. In such a set-up, those who have peculiar excellences are more likely to find their way when they have entry by doing something they can do well, and then proceeding to their more particular interests, and by being accepted for *what* they can do.

Academic schooling, of course, could be chosen by those with academic talents. Obviously, schools would be better off if unencumbered by sullen uninterested bodies. But the main use of academic teaching should be for those already busy in the sciences and the professions, who need academic courses along the way to acquire further knowledge. Cooper Union in New York City used to fulfill this function very well.

Of course, in such a set-up, employers would themselves provide ancillary academic training. In my opinion, this ancillary schooling would do more than any other single thing to give blacks, rurals, and other culturally deprived youth a fairer entry and a chance for advancement. As we have seen, there is no correlation *on the job* between competence and prior schooling.

This leads to another problem. Educationally, schooling on the job is usually superior to academic schooling, but the political and moral consequences of such a system are ambiguous. At present, a youth is hired because of his *credentials*, rather than for his actual skill. This system allows a measure of free-market democracy. However, if he is to be schooled on the job, he must be hired essentially for his promise. Such a system can lead to company paternalism like Japanese capitalism. On the other hand, if the young have options and they are allowed to organize and to criticize, on-the-job education is the quickest way to workers' management which, in my opinion, is the only effective democracy.

University education—liberal arts and the principles of the professions—should be reserved only for adults who already know something, and who have something about which to philosophize. Otherwise, as Plato pointed out, such "education" is just mere verbalizing.

To provide a protective and life-nourishing environment for children up through age twelve, Summerhill is an adequate model. I think Summerhill can be easily adapted to urban conditions. Probably, an even better model would be the Athenian pedagogue touring the city with his charges; but for this to work out, the streets and the working-places of the city will have to be made safer and more available than it is likely they will be. The prerequisite of city-planning is that children be able to *use* the city; for no city is governable if it does not grow citizens who feel that that city is theirs.

The goal of elementary pedagogy is a very modest one: a small child should be able, under his own steam, to poke interestedly into whatever goes on; and he should be able, through observation, through questions, and through practical imitation, to get something out of such poking around. In our society this is what happens at home pretty well up to age four; but after that, such random poking around becomes forbiddingly difficult.

*   *   *

I have often spelled out this program of incidental education, and I have found no takers. Curiously, I get the most respectful if wistful attention at teachers' colleges, even though what I propose is quite impossible under present administration. Teachers *know* how much they are wasting the children's time, and teachers understand that my proposals are fairly conservative.

However, in a general audience the response is incredulity. Against all evidence, people are convinced that what we are now doing must make sense or we wouldn't be doing it. It doees not help if I point out that in dollars and cents it might be cheaper—and it would certainly be more productive—to eliminate most schools and have the community itself provide more of the education. Yet the majority in a general audience are willing to admit that they themselves got very little out of *their* school years. Occasionally, an old reactionary business-man agrees with me enthusiastically that book-learning isn't worth a penny.

Among radical students, my proposals are met by a sullen silence. They want Student Power, and for the most part, they are unwilling to answer whether they are authentically students at all. I think they're brainwashed. Naturally, it makes no difference to them if they demand "University Reform," or if the University is shut down altogether.

Instead of Student Power, what they should be demanding is (a) a more open entry into society, and (b) that education money should be spent more usefully, and (c) that licensing and hiring should be handled without consideration of irrelevant diplomas; and so forth. Youth Power can make the authentic demand for the right to take part in initiating and deciding the functions of society that concern them, as well as the right to govern their own lives— which are nobody else's business. Bear in mind that I am speaking of youths between age 17 and 25. At all other times in man's history, these individuals would already have found their places in the real world.

Nathan W. Ackerman is recognized as a foremost authority in the field of family therapy. As Director of the Professional Program of the Family Institute, he trains psychologists and psychiatrists in methods of treating problems between parent and child, and husband and wife.

Dr. Ackerman serves as Clinical Professor of Psychiatry at Columbia University, and Visiting Professor at the Albert Einstein College of Medicine. He has lectured at universities and hospitals in the United States, and before university medical groups and professional societies throughout the world.

He has been accorded special awards by the Association for Improvement of Mental Health by the Eastern Group Psychotherapy Association.

He is the author of FAMILY THERAPY, PSYCHODYNAMICS OF FAMILY LIFE, TREATING THE TROUBLED FAMILY.

Nathan W. Ackerman

It is now almost a half century since the educator, A. S. Neill, founded the Summerhill school—"a radical approach to child rearing," he called it. Across the years, some commentators have characterized it as a landmark, a turning point in the history of progressive education; others have chalked it off as a Utopian bubble. How shall we look upon it today?

To take an arbitrary stand for or against Summerhill would, in my view, be the height of folly. What is important is not the right or wrong of Neill's views on education but the fact that this experiment took place. In the setting of our time, we are bound to ask: What is the relevance of these educational principles for the utterly changed world of today? Are the educational problems with which Neill wrestled long ago still live, pertinent issues for the crisis of our time.

Education is a bridge between the individual, the family, and society. It is a bridge between the old and the new. Learning is the tool by which a person adapts to the ever-shifting historical equilibrium of "continuity within change and change within continuity."

The education of the young cannot be considered in a social vacuum, but only within the context of a particular way of life. The issue is education for *what*, for what tasks, for what kinds of people, and for what kind of society. The rearing and education of children is a challenge that must be faced for each successive phase in the evolution of human society and conceptualized in a different way for each generation.

With lightning speed, we have moved from a stable culture to an unstable one. Revolutionary changes are sweeping the world.

"In a few short years the solidarity of the world order has vapor-ized into a nightmare of uncertainty."[1] The impact of "cultural lag" is felt everywhere. Amidst this turmoil of revolutionary change, we are facing the deepest educational crisis of all time. The controversy in our schools cannot be separated from the political conflicts of the community. The unrest and revolt of youth on the university campuses is seeping down to infect the lower schools. The problems of child care and education take on quite new dimensions. The chaos of our time bears witness to the crucial importance of the question: Education for what kind of society? Says Jules Henry:[2]

> "The paradox of the human condition is ex-pressed more in education than elsewhere in the human culture." . . . Is educational process in-tended to fetter or free?" . . . "The fettering of the mind while we set the spirit free or the fettering of the spirit as we free the mind is an abiding para-dox of civilization."[2]

The present day crisis in education brings into bold relief problems which Neill faced almost 50 years ago. Order and dis-cipline vs. freedom; understanding vs. punishment; self-regulation vs. authoritarian control; participation in the shaping of educa-tional policy vs. conformity to an imposed system.

In a recent number of *Life* magazine the issues are sharply etched.

> "Is the main purpose of education to teach the skills to live in a fast changing society? Is educa-

[1] Hansen, W. "Environment and Design," *ETC*, Autumn 1955, p. 19
[2] Henry, Jules *Culture Against Man* Random House, 1963, pp. 285-6

*tion just a tool for fitting us into the system? . . .
Authority demands conformity, conformity leads
to routine, and routine produces boredom. Youth
takes the position that adults don't understand
the dehumanization, the automation of the school
system.*

*"The students want to discover who they are
and the school wants to help them make something of themselves. They want to know where
they are; the school wants to help them get somewhere. They want to learn how to live with themselves; the school wants to teach them how to get
along with others. They want to learn what is
right for themselves; the school wants to teach
them the responses that will earn them rewards
in the classroom and the social situation."*[3]

In the cry of youth for involvement, for a voice in molding educational policy, for a curriculum that is relevant to the critical
problems of contemporary society, parents and educators respond
with dramatically divided sentiment. Partly, the older generation
says: Youth lacks discipline, ambition, spiritual and moral fiber,
responsibility, manners, and respect for authority. Partly, the
older generation extends to youth a deep sympathy for its search
for new values and a new kind of education. Youth is smart,
aware, honest, and yet turns to violence.

In the 1920's, Summerhill was a brave, pioneering and yet
lonely experiment in the care of children. It was an impassioned
protest, a fierce reaction against the incompetence and cruelty of
traditional teaching systems. Acting as a catalyst, it evoked a

[3] *Life,* May 23, 1969

stream of controversy concerning the philosophy of child care which continues to this day.

Neill committed his entire being to the creation of a school that fits the child, his image of the child. The very core of his educational approach is a fundamental respect for the power of the child's curiosity and interest. The traditional concern with work in the classroom and lessons governed by educational requirements is subordinated. The child learns by playing. The criteria that really count are happiness, security, balance, and sociability.

The Summerhill school is a dream of raising and educating children in love and in freedom. In such an atmosphere the child holds head and heart together, develops a reverence of life and learns to love rather than turning to attitudes of hate and anti-life. The ideal seems to be a "nature child" in a natural environment.

The philosophy which underlies the Summerhill approach to child education reveals a fierce dichotomy. Neill loves children; he indicts parents and society. The child is good; the parents and the social system are bad—they are, in fact, stupid. Neill's aim is to bring happiness to some few children, not to reform family and society.

In his view, the child is innately good, wise, and realistic. It is the nature of the child to seek happiness, to find interest. The right of youth is to "play and play and play;" this is the royal road to learning. Fantasy is the indispensable bridge to reality. "In true play, the child is intent, responsive, unhurried, completely involved—there's a lovely seriousness about it."[4]

Conventional book learning separates the heart from the head; it separates the child from his emotions; it disciplines the child above the neck. Traditional academic learning is coercive and punishing; it suffocates the child and teaches him to hate. Only

[4] Leonard, George B. *Education and Ecstasy*, Delacorte Press, N.Y., 1968

in an atmosphere of affection and freedom can a child emerge into a whole being. Above all else, the relation of teacher and pupil must be governed by an uncompromising honesty and sincerity. The goal for the child is to work joyfully and to live abundantly. In this setting there is no room for punishment. This is poison for the vital spirit of the child.

And yet, freedom does not mean license. Freedom leaves off and license begins when the child encroaches on the rights of others. You can be as free as you like, as long as you do not interfere with another person's freedom. When boy and girl are raised together there is pride in the body, not shame. "There is never a problem child, there are only problem parents, only a problem humanity." "It is a race between believers in deadness and believers in life." This is the core of Neill's philosophy of child education.

The value of the Summerhill experiment lies least of all in its answers. In fact, Summerhill provides remarkably few answers. What really counts is a new understanding of old problems. A close examination of this unique experience in child education places a beacon light on the issues of contemporary education.

As we have said, Neill loves children; he indicts parents and society. But these same parents were once children and many of the former pupils of Summerhill are now parents. A parent after all is a child's first teacher. Does it make sense to rescue the child and do away with the parents? This is somehow reminiscent of that rare obstetrical dilemma, whom to save, mother or baby. In the long view, there is only one way: to save our children, we must also save parents, family, and society. Where Neill stopped, we must now begin—to reform family and society.

For me Summerhill is a poetic vision. As such, I am all for it. Who can quarrel with the idea? Who would want to? How to reach out toward it is the question. In life we strive toward the ideal, and yet must come to terms with the real. As a psychiatrist who has devoted a lifetime to a quest for understanding the relations of parents and children, I know first hand the need for respecting a child's nature, for cherishing and nourishing his spirit, for supporting a free, warm, happy expansion into the world of people. Keeping heart and head together is of the essence. It is the only way to unfold the child's capacity for love and for learning. How to do it in this age of technology and alienation is the real question.

Surely we cannot grasp the problem by looking to the child alone. We must examine every aspect of the child's environment. What forces in the community nourish the child's growth and learning? What forces stultify it? Ultimately, the aim must be to create a sound, healthy family, school and community environment within which a child may maximize his potentials for creative development, and by so doing ripen into a secure, wholesome person who makes his full contribution to the well being of society.

The cure of man's ills cannot be conventional "success;" it cannot be therapy. In the final analysis, it must be dedication of a kind that transforms the existing twisted, sick, human environment into one that builds integrity and joy into the patterns of family and community. It is only within such an environment that we may hope to fulfill the potentials of man's nature, not just those of the child but of all of us and at every stage of the life cycle. The task of the new education is monumental. It imposes an infinitude of problems. To say we have not yet found the solution is the understatement of the age.

Surely it is not possible to grasp the Summerhill method apart from the man. Neill, the man, has lived his message as an individual, as a family person, as a teacher, and as a student. In talking of the man, we can do no better than to quote a simple, eloquent statement of the British government inspectors.

> "The headmaster is a man of conviction and sincerity. His faith and patience must be inexhaustible. He has the rare power of being a strong personality without dominating—he has a sense of humor, a warmth for humanity and a strong common sense. What cannot be doubted is that a piece of fascinating, educational research is going on here."[5]

Those who have had the good fortune to know Neill personally attest to his charisma. The openness, candor and charm of his personality has had a hypnotic effect on visitors to his school.

A noted educator, Goodwin Watson, who lived for a time in Neill's home, says the following:

> "Neill had the vision, courage and practical skills to explore another path. No other educator whom I know has as much that is stimulating and important to say to American parents and teachers at this moment."

Henry Miller offers this opinion:

> "I know of no other educator in the Western world who compares to A. S. Neill. It seems to me that he stands alone. Summerhill is a tiny ray of light in a world of darkness. Its aim is to create

[5] *Summerhill*, p. 83

> *happy, contented people, not cultural misfits dedi-*
> *cated to war, insanity and canned knowledge."*

From another angle, Erich Fromm says:

> *"I believe in Neill's work as a seed which will*
> *germinate. Within time his ideals will become*
> *generally recognized in a new society in which*
> *man himself and his own unfolding are the su-*
> *preme aim of all social effort."*

The message from Summerhill is an earthy message from an earthy man; it is a spiritual message from a spiritual man. In the rearing of children, join the heart and head, help them to feel as well as to think. Let them discover their bodies and other bodies in a warm, free, spontaneous way. Let them find the joys of play amidst easy, natural surroundings. Support them to live abundantly. Love the child and the child will love humanity.

Does the Summerhill philosophy stand or fall by its end-product, the kind of adult persons the pupils grow into? I do not think so. Many considerations argue against the usefulness of this approach as the sole criterion. The factors involved are too complex and varied to allow retrospective assessment. Among these many complicating considerations there is, for example, the selective nature of the pupil population. Generally, only those children whose families could afford the tuition were admitted. Except for an occasional scholarship, poor children coming from poor parents could not be included in the Summerhill community. The children came from a relatively few social classes and ethnic and cultural backgrounds. They were drawn from a small part of the Western world and from very few countries. At the outset, many of the children admitted to Summerhill were disturbed children coming from disturbed families. The emotional problems of these children were linked to disturbances of learning. Later, it is true, the proportion of disturbed children was reduced.

There are further questions. What kinds of families send their children into exile at a relatively early age, even to a school like Summerhill? There is the special complication of the relative isolation of the school from home, family, and surrounding community. We have no way of knowing how many of these children were ever re-united with their families. Neill tells us that his successes were mainly with those children who came from good homes. One would surely want to know what happened to the children who came from bad homes.

Regardless of the handicaps with which some of these children were burdened, it is indeed impressive to read the characterization of the Summerhill pupils by the great British government inspectors.

> *"They are full of life and zest, there is no sign of boredom or apathy. The children hold an attitude of deep affection for the school. They are ꞌfriendly, easy and natural. They have a lack of shyness and self-consciousness. They are very easy, pleasant people to get on with. The system encourages initiative, responsibility and integrity."*[6]

The alumni of Summerhill have turned into artists, musicians, designers, a few scientists and mathematicians. Mainly, these children lean toward some kind of original and creative activity. One is certainly impressed by the pupils' own devotion to the school. Neill said he cares not if an alumnus turns into a shoe-

[6] *Summerhill*, p. 84

maker or mechanic. Yet these children seem to have been well served by Neill's philosophy, "to discover the ability to work positively and to live positively."

Inevitably, with this system of education there are some costs and some casualties. Once again, to quote the British government inspectors:

> *"On the whole the results of this system are unimpressive—the children work with a willing interest that is most refreshing but their achievements are meager."*

Do these children acquire the needed basic skills to cope with the problems of society? Do they develop a true love of learning? Or do they learn only along avenues that provide an immediate reward in excitement and pleasure?

With an overriding emphasis on creative play, do these children lack guidance and discipline? Do they fail to respect private property? Do they perhaps learn the responsibility of work at a relatively late age. Says Neill: "A sane civilization would not ask a child to work until the age of 18." There are many critics, including myself, who would sharply dissent from this view. Granting the principle that a child's play is serious business and that one learns by playing, there remains the question how do we join work and play and where does play end and work begin.

*   *   *

A close reading of Summerhill discloses some curious paradoxes and contradictions. The first of these relates to love and freedom as cure. According to Neill, it is the loving environment of the school that heals the hurt child. It is not Neill's psychotherapeutic session, the "private lesson" that cures; it is rather the warm acceptance, respect and affection provided by the school community.

In the fields of child education and guidance, the concept of love as cure has been asserted again and again; it has become something of a cliche. Over and over in reports on children we find the statement "this child needs warmth and affection." The formula is TLC, "tender loving care." It has been an underlying assumption that where the parents fail to give love to the child, the teacher and therapist must provide the antidote.

In a paper called "Psychotherapy and Giving Love,"[7] I discussed the question in the following vein. Giving love cannot be a technique, nor a device, nor a strategy. It must be genuine and sincere; it must be the real thing. Just as a starved person is least able to stomach food, so too, a person starved for love is least able to digest it.

There are two related issues: Is the child ready to receive the loving? Can the teacher or therapist give it? When a child is emotionally starved, he cannot accept loving until his underlying fears, suspicion, and anger are first melted down. Often, such a child is unable to ask for love; instead he steals it or takes it by force.

A child most hungry for love is riddled with guilt, is hostile or depressed, and often takes recourse to outbursts of aggression. Such a child, fearing trickery and betrayal, hits out first. He lashes out at the very person making the offering of love. Impelled by a fear of humiliation and pain, a deprived child is apt to feel, "the hostility of others brings out the best in me." This is, "a bond of unfriendliness," with a vengeance. A child of this kind hangs a

[7] Ackerman, Nathan W. Psychotherapy and Giving Love *Psychiatry*, Vol. 7, No. 2, May, 1944.

sign outside of her bedroom door: "Beware, high voltage! If you come too close, you will be electrocuted." The child's motive is to ward off the so-called affection of her mother. Obviously, one cannot offer a handshake to a high tension wire; one must first turn off the current.

A child, immature and impulsive, must often be protected from injuring himself or those about him. In the case of an emotionally starved child who hits out first, it is useful to apply passive physical restraint. The explosion of uncontrolled aggression must be curbed before such a child becomes ready to accept an offering of love. Passive physical restraint, applied when necessary, by a responsible adult, need not be bitter nor vindictive, but it must be firm; the child needs to be reminded that he does not possess omnipotent power. The issue is not so much the act of restraint but the how and why of it. Where a child interprets restraint as punishment, this need not be the adult's intention. The child may simply misunderstand. Across time, the child comes to appreciate that the true motive of the adult is protection, not punishment.

One cannot help but wonder as to the relevance of this lesson for the control of violence in our time. Somehow violence, instead of being recognized simply for what it is—a destructive and dangerous response to fright, frustration and despair—comes to be viewed as an ideology, a social cause in its own right.

I once treated a difficult child who assaulted me with a wood plank pitted with sharp nails. I restrained the child physically. He screamed as if I were killing him. He then began to bite my hand. When I stopped this, he proceeded to spit. I then offered him the palm of my hand; whereupon unexpectedly, he turned my hand about and kissed the back of it. He seemed suddenly to discover that I was not really killing him but only protecting him and myself. With this discovery, his violence abruptly turned to a gesture of love.

The other side of the equation is the question of the teacher's ability to give love. Is the teacher tendering an offer of genuine love, or is it a gesture? In many classrooms today, a teacher pats a child's head, addresses the child in endearing terms, "darling" or "honey." One is reminded of the Hollywood style where people indiscriminately address strangers as *darling* and *honey*. How far is this a true loving? How far is it rather a pose, a gesture, a gimmick with a concealed motive of controlling or obligating the child, a tactic for bribing the child to good behavior? How far does it reflect the teacher's need to seduce and bind the child against a show of rebellion and hostility? How far does it signify the teacher's need to aggrandize the self or to show up the inadequacy of the child's parents. To the extent that this is a true expression of warmth and affection, both teacher and child are enriched thereby, and the child may likely respond with greater receptivity to learning. To the extent that the offering is a false, hypocritical gesture, it will complicate the relationship, stir resentment and bring a further block in learning.

Emotional disturbance, coupled with learning difficulty, is not a simple deficiency disease. It is not merely a question of feeding the child "love vitamins." The suspicious child who fears exposure to humiliation, pain, and injury and lashes out, must first have an opportunity to learn new feelings and attitudes towards adults before he can trust or assimilate an offering of love.

An exaggerated or inappropriate demand for love, may not actually be an asking for genuine affection. Instead, it may be a testing of the adult's control, the urge of the child to usurp power, a craving for domination, a concealed reproach, a placation or disarming of the adult. Basically, this is a denial of mistrust and hostility, rather than a true asking for love. It is necessary that the adult recognizes the difference. Let us face it: grown-ups do not have a boundless, unconditional love of children; all loving is conditional. The notion of an unconditional love of children is, I believe, a myth which I have characterized as "the delusion of the boundless breast."

A related problem emerges in the Summerhill philosophy of a total ban on coercion and punishment. Neill's taboo on corporal punishment is absolute. Several questions arise here. How consistent is the implementation of this principle? Is there perhaps some confusion between the application of appropriate controls, physical and moral, and the loathing and rejection of the motive of adult retaliation? There seem to be some contradictions.

There are, in fact, at Summerhill some ground rules to assure physical safety and to protect against encroachment on the rights of others. "All cases of bullying will be severely dealt with." For some breaches of conduct there are penalties. Curiously enough, for others—for example, for stealing—there are sometimes actual rewards in money. This is a paradoxical attempt to undercut the need to steal by the surprise tactic of rewarding it. Mainly, the penalties are in the form of deprivation of privileges; for example, no movies.

I, for one, view deprivation of privileges as a weak, self defeating discipline. The punishment bears no relation to the crime. It is a case of closing the barn doors after the cow has left. A core theme in Neill's philosophy is an aversion to authoritarian control. (Neill's own father was a headmaster, a severe disciplinarian; in class, Neill suffered frequent switchings from his teachers.) It is as if Neill sees the adult mainly through the eyes of the child. He joins the child's suspicion of the adult. He over-identifies with the child in indicting the adult. All adult control is suspect because it is immediately equated with the presumed motive of punishment. It seems to me that when an adult responds to a child's destructive aggression with a spontaneous slap or a genuine burst of anger, or a firm, non-punitive physical restraint, this is more natural, more honest, more effective, and less hurtful than the deprivation of privileges.

With respect to the principle of self-regulation there are also some subtle inconsistencies. At Summerhill, there is student participation in decision-making in the form of general school meetings. Without doubt, this deepens the child's sense of involvement, strengthens his feeling of responsibility toward the school community. Yet there are reservations and distinct limits to the principle of pupil control. There are restrictions relating to the rights of others, and the need to respect private property. Neill himself raises a big hullabaloo if the children misuse his shop or damage his tools. There is a constant reminder that freedom does not mean license. Neill frankly admits the perennial conflict between the individual and society. On occasion he makes some flat contradictions. "I am no authority to be feared, I am their equal—yet I am the boss." There is a plaguing question here. Does Neill go too far in his empathic identification with the child and then find that he must back down? In his insistence on being "pal" to his pupils, does he abdicate a position of authority? Is he then compelled under provocation to reassert it? In this aspect of his educational ideology there seems to be some definite ambiguity.

A different problem emerges in the conceptualization of the role of the adult in the Summerhill community. He has to be teacher, parent, and therapist, all rolled into one. For the adult to be all things to all children is a little much. Under ordinary life conditions the responsibility for child rearing is a shared one, shared by parent, teacher, and society. Each of these has a special set of caretaking duties to fulfill for a young child. Parent, teacher, and community are expected to join and collaborate in appropriate ways in the interests of the well-being of children. At Summerhill, what family and society are expected to do for a child are piled on the teacher's back. For one poor teacher this is a burden too great to bear. Therefore, it is no great surprise to discover some inconsistencies and failures within this educational system.

To be sure, there is a historic background, an understandable explanation, for the merging of the several roles within the one person. When children are exiled from their homes and placed in boarding school, the teacher must stand *in loco parentis*. There is an implicit assumption that the child's parents have already failed, both as parents and as teachers. As a consequence, many such children are afflicted with emotional disorders and learning blocks. Following the psychoanalytic traditions of Anna Freud and August Aichorn, Summerhill gives up on the parents. The responsible adults at the school must now take on the whole job of child rearing. They must now assume the burden of repairing the damage inflicted on the child's growth by family and community.

Beyond the creation of new life, the proper role of the parent is to insure the child's survival, to nourish the child's growth, to love and socialize the child, to train the child for his appropriate position and role within the family, and to provide the link with the surrounding community and culture.

The role of the teacher is to inculcate a love of learning and to impart the knowledge and skills which the child needs, to unfold his capacities in the larger society. The teacher carries out his role in a complementary partnership with parents and community.

The role of the therapist is a specialized one, to reduce an excess of anxiety, to dissolve out emotional blocks to personal development and social learning, to foster more effective levels of coping with conflict, to repair damage to self-esteem, to enhance relationships.

The role of the community is to support parent, family and teacher in the execution of their appropriate responsibilities. As the child matures, the community must provide opportunities for effective integration into the social system and the culture.

In the special circumstance in which all of these responsibilities are foisted on the back of the teacher, the inevitable result is an over-load that can only lead to distortion. It is easy to identify and trace some of these complications. For example, at Summerhill the teacher struggles with a 24-hour job. He is relieved of his duties altogether, only when he leaves the school on holiday. There is no personal privacy. There is continuous struggle over the right of the teachers to have closed doors. A teacher must not have his own children in the school where he teaches. At the end of the school year, Neill and his wife find themselves utterly exhausted.

What, exactly, must be the sacrifice of the grownup? When a teacher gives more than he has in his emotional bank, he is depleted; he is in a state of spiritual bankruptcy; he must inevitably be irritable and resentful. The impact on the children can, then, only be a noxious one.

An imbalance in the relations of child and adult seems to creep into the school environment. It is child centered; it is molded to suit the needs of children. But how about the needs of adults? Neill takes the position that the grown-up must make the sacrifice. Is he doing penance? Is he trying to make up for the hurts imposed on the child by parents and society? Can this really be done? Should adults immolate themselves for the child?

Granted the parents have often exploited and scapegoated their children; granted that rigid, authoritarian parents have often abused and tied their child to strict conformity—do we solve the problem by turning the tables and making the adult world submit to the demands of children? There is real risk here of disorganization and anarchy. The answer is not self-sacrifice for the adult; it is, rather, the creation of a true balance between the generations while keeping faith with the natural differences of child and adult.

The various philosophies of child rearing and education seem to polarize themselves between a prime allegiance to the heart or to the head. In a sense, the dichotomies of order and discipline versus freedom, punishment versus understanding, and authority and control versus love and self-regulation reflect this basic split between the heart and the head. Shall a child be governed from the head down or from the heart up? It is this tendency to make "permissiveness" or control an either/or issue that divides the world of grownups in its approach to systems of child rearing and education.

We have experienced in a profound way the maiming and mutilating effects of authoritarian control on child development and on the child's capacity to learn. We have discovered the pathogenic consequences of a divorce of heart and head. We have learned the harm of inappropriate permissiveness, the distortions resulting from the adult's abdication of authority: an excess anxiety in the child—sometimes even sheer terror—or an eruption of anarchy and violence. Need it be all head and no heart, or all heart and no head? Is this not again a problem of keeping heart and head together, and yet striving for the appropriate balance?

The relative isolation of the Summerhill school from home and community poses special difficulties. When family and society abandon a child and, even more, when a child abandons family and society, it is most difficult to restore the connection. If, for whatever reason, a child is rejected by his parents, the ultimate answer does not necessarily rest in placement of the child in a boarding-school, or in a residential treatment center. Either of these implies a giving up on family.

It is parents who make the gift of life to children. Making a baby is easy; caring for it is quite another matter. Child care is a shared responsibility. When parents and family fail, we must find ways to reform society and restore the integrity of family living. A healthy integration of a child into a society is possible only on the foundation of a healthy integration within the family group. Where the child's fit with family fails, the child's fit with his peer society also fails. In the long view, the isolation of a child from home and community in a special school, even if that happens to be Summerhill, is no solution.

Placement of a child in a special school at age five or age six means disruption of the basic emotional union of child and parent. Healthy union means healthy individuation. An incomplete or twisted union with parents brings a twisted pattern of individuation; it leads to alienation and fragmentation of relationships.

Summerhill is a kind of "island culture," separated from the surrounding community by an imaginary wall. In order for Summerhill to preserve its integrity, its distinctive values, and its relationship patterns, it must provide "a protective envelope." It must fence out the potentially invasive forces of a larger culture of which it is a part. Can this really be done?

An island culture is able only in some part to maintain its integrity through isolation. Summerhill's imaginary wall is surely penetrable. Inevitably, there must be some communication, some interchange of influence in both directions, from the community to Summerhill, and from Summerhill to the community. Of this there is clear evidence, as for example Neill's necessary concessions to the community regarding the freedom of sexual expression of the Summerhill children.

In their emotional development, with whom can these children establish identity connections? In what way do the children experience togetherness? There is little doubt that Neill lived his values honestly and in depth, but Neill's values were largely the values of a child. He saw adults through the eyes of a child. He established and maintained a world for children. It would seem that the Summerhill children identified with Neill, because he identified with them. Through this union, the children were able to cultivate deep and warm relationships with their peers. It is my hunch that the Summerhill community is predominantly a peer society.

Arthur Miller, the playwright, asked this question:

> "How may a man make of the outside world a home? How and in what ways must he struggle? What must he strive to change and overcome within himself and outside himself if he is to find the safety, the surroundings of love, the ease of soul, the sense of identity and honor which all men have connected in their memories with the idea of family?"

In significant measure, the children of Summerhill found the sense of family within their school community. It is this experience of true togetherness that perhaps gave these children some immunity against the cold, depersonalizing, dehumanizing forces of the larger culture.

*   *   *

The understanding of learning difficulties in a child poses a subtle and immensely complicated challenge. The contributing factors are multi-determined: the individual quality of the child, the family, the school, and the community. A long time ago, I served as psychiatric consultant to the Hunter College Educational Clinic. The professional staff of this clinic and I wrestled together with the problem of learning failures in children. During eight years of operation of this educational clinic, 250 children with learning difficulties and associated behavior problems were studied. During my tenure as psychiatric consultant, we made a special effort to understand the correlation of family experience and failures of learning. We found that before the child fails in the classroom, he has already failed to learn within his own home. Mother and father have already failed as teachers. To illustrate:

A bright, eight-year old girl suffers a reading retardation. She is demure, ladylike, ingratiating, and frightened. The pressure toward academic achievement makes her uneasy and depressed; she feels "dumb," and shows great anxiety concerning bad marks in school. When she fails in school, she feels she is "bringing terrible news home to mother." She has an intense need to win her mother's approval, and tries to buy that approval with submission. She distrusts mother, is resistive to mother's nourishment, and has a feeding problem. At the same time, she has learned to manipulate mother. She exhibits intense separation anxiety and has deep-lying fears of death. The mother feels guilty about the child's birth. She experienced profound anxieties about a possible birth defect or deformity. Following the child's birth, she thought the baby was too passive, almost like a "dead baby." The child was too good, "she clung to her mother." The mother needed to feel the child as helpless. She emphasized achievement in masculine terms.

Both parents were hypocritical and deceitful in their relations with the child and with each other. There was a submerged mistrust and hostility between them. The mother pretended to support father's masculinity, but perceived it as an act. In a sly way she undercut the father's masculinity, and ended up as boss. She assumed a protective posture toward the child as if guarding her from father's irritability. This child was kept an infant. Her confidence was severly injured; her growth and learning were stunted.

A boy of six years, has an I.Q. of 141. He has no interest in learning, and refuses to do school work. He manifests extreme fear when confronted with a learning challenge. He exhibits acute separation anxiety. He resists sleep until exhausted. He has a rocking ritual. He is extremely negativistic. A teacher describes him as tense, tied in knots. He has little contact with children except when urged to tease them. In his early development, he suffered from eczema. He wet and soiled till the age of five. To avoid accidents, the mother pushed him to the toilet. There was a battle of wills between them. The child rebelled against schedules. He fought bathing and dressing. It required force to get him out of the house. At night, he called continuously for his mother. At times, the mother exhausted from this battle, slipped slyly out of the home. This child became absorbed in fantasy play.

Mother is a lonely, isolated person, with marked feelings of inferiority. She is extremely dependent and is moderately depressed. As a child, she herself had worried about school work, and was particularly anxious about examinations. Father is a perfectionist and is critical about both himself and his wife. He also felt lonely and unloved. He was unable to tolerate noise or distraction, and was given to violent outbursts. Mother and father were mutually dependent and denied the undercurrent of hostile emotion between them. In the first phase of their marriage, the wife mothered the husband. They removed themselves from extended family and community, and took care of one another. This delicate balance between them was disrupted when they had children. Theirs is a child whose emotional and social development is arrested. He experiences himself as helplessly dependent on mother, but is suspicious and vulnerable. He resists his mother's control, feeling it as coercion. He resorts to outright aggression. The resulting learning failure is pervasive.

The problems of learning failure are dramatically highlighted in children of black families living in socio-economic destitution. The deprived child of an impoverished black family exhibits learning disorders in extreme form. He experiences an appalling dearth of positive stimulation. He is emotionally stultified, oppressed, depressed, isolated. He feels despair. His hope is crushed. He is frightened, suspicious and angry. In episodic outbursts, he makes an aggressive assault on his surroundings. He bashes his head against the outer world which seems not to care about him. He is frozen emotionally. He is retarded in learning. He suffers a kind of marasmus of his creative faculties.

The destitute black family is sometimes viewed as the disorganized, depressed, "dirty" fringe of the larger community. The Negro family of the ghetto does not live; it exists. "Life is not lived; it is undergone."[8] It is small wonder that black children, the product of an oppressed way of life in the ghetto, suffer profound difficulties of learning.

When an innocent child is emotionally maimed, and arrested in his learning, whom shall we blame, the child, himself, his parents, his family, his teacher, or the social community at large? Society either turns its face away, or points an accusing finger at the parents. The parents blame the teachers; the teachers blame the parents. All of them together blame the "system." Were we to neglect the physical care of the children as we neglect their mind and spirit, we would consider ourselves mad. This is not merely a tragic failure for a few children, it is a profound loss for all of humanity.

*   *   *

Do human understanding, creativity and learning depend on a special talent or gift? Some children display more of these qualities, some less. It is more a question of who has what talent, how much, and under what conditions it may be brought to flower.

[8] Hertha Riese, *Heal the Hurt Child,* Univ. of Chicago Press, 1962

Why is it that so much original talent is aborted even before it is born?

Putting aside the question of rare and special gifts, the fact is that human understanding, creativity, and learning are universal powers. To begin with, each of us has these powers. Inherent in each and every child, there is an infinity of creation. To be sure, among children at birth the diversities are legion, but the dormant capacities are there. The possibilities of development are almost boundless. The realization of these potentials hinges both on the inner child, and on the relations of the child with his environment. The actualization of these capacities is of the greatest urgency.

But here lies the rub. The potentials of understanding, creativity, and learning, if they are to be actualized, must not only be discovered, but nourished and practiced. If we do not call these capacities into use, if we do not cultivate them, they simply do not emerge. Without care and stimulation to new growth, they wither away; they atrophy from disuse. Do we in our homes, schools and communities prize these basic resources? Do we evoke them? Do we feed them? Do we provide for them a rich culture in which to grow? The answer is clearly no. We are guilty of neglect. The latent abilities of children are barely stirred to life.

To an alarming extent the emotional growth of many children is stunted. The potentials for understanding, for creative living and learning are choked off in the early years of life. By their very nature, children have a native capacity and craving for expansive growth. They express this in their sparkling spontaneity, in their bright, bubbly, vivid curiosity about the world that surrounds them. Within a few years, this interest, this rich imaginative reaching out becomes cowed and deadened. The urge to explore shrinks; it dries up from sheer lack of exercise. These children soon turn into dull, drab, inhibited, conforming citizens. They lose their spark and animation. They cease to grow—or they explode with violence.

The stultified, twisted growth of these children is the result of disorders of family life, inadequate educational systems, and the failure of understanding on the part of the larger community. These children suffer from a deficiency of nourishment, of understanding, of love. Their spontaneous play and curiosity are crushed; they are victimized by coercion and restriction of expression. The heart of the child becomes split. He becomes depersonalized and dehumanized.

How shall we attack this problem, this tragic loss and destruction of basic human capacities? Is there an antidote? Surely, to succor a handful of child victims, "to give happiness to some few children," is a pathetically small endeavor. Important in its own right, it must still be counted as a minor accomplishment when compared with the length and breadth of the challenge for all of humanity.

Studies now emerge which break new ground in the areas of child development and learning,[9] in family life[10] and child care,[11] in systems of education and parent-teacher collaboration, and finally in the evolution of a creative community which cares about its parents and children.

Learning disorders and underachievement are a consequence of a sick family, a sick school system, a sick community. So, too, are the evils of mental illness, crime, and war. In the long view, if we are to neutralize this enormous human waste, we must transform the environment of man. We must evolve a sound, healthy community within which man may grow to his full height. Only now do we begin to envisage what a truly healthy human community might be.

[9] *Carnegie Quarterly,* Vol. 12, No. 1, Winter 1969
[10] Ackerman, Nathan W. *The Psychodynamics of Family Life,* Basic Books, N.Y. 1958
[11] Ackerman, Nathan W. *Treating the Troubled Family,* Basic Books, N.Y., 1966

Erich Fromm is internationally known as a psychologist and writer. His book, THE ART OF LOVING, *achieved world-wide fame and has been translated into eighteen languages. His major works deal with psychological as well as philosophical and current issues faced by man:* ESCAPE FROM FREEDOM, MAN FOR HIMSELF, PSYCHOANALYSIS AND RELIGION, BEYOND THE CHAINS OF ILLUSION, MAY MAN PREVAIL?, YOU SHALL BE AS GODS, THE REVOLUTION OF HOPE.

Having been granted his doctorate in philosophy at Heidelberg in 1922, he undertook psychiatric training at the Berlin Institute of Psychoanalysis from which he graduated in 1931.

Dr. Fromm heads the Department of Psychoanalysis of the Medical School of the National University of Mexico, and also holds a professorship of Psychology at New York University. He has been a guest lecturer at Columbia University, Yale University, The New School for Social Research, and in many other halls of learning.

He wrote the foreword to A. S. Neill's SUMMERHILL: A RADICAL APPROACH TO CHILD REARING.

Erich Fromm

A. S. Neill's book, *Summerhill*, has had a remarkable career. In the ten years since its publication, it has become very popular in educational institutions in spite of an educational philosophy which is thoroughly in disagreement with the status quo.

A. S. Neill presented a theory that he believed would make people happier and that would help parents bring up children for whom *being* more—not *having* more nor *using* more—would be the aim of life. Proof that the existing educational system is wrong-headed and harmful has since been amply provided by the campus rebellion, an international rebellion involving most countries of Europe and America.

What is the student rebellion all about? The phenomenon is somewhat different within each country. In some, it represents socialist demands; in others, a fight for greater student participation in the deliberations and the decision-making of the university establishment. In these struggles, some groups have rejected violence; in others, various degrees of force have been employed. In some cases, institutional methods have been attacked; in others, particular individuals have been damned. Yet behind all these apparent differences, all the marching, sitting, and shouting students have something in common: *they are all experiencing a deep hunger for life*. They feel that their education is being bureaucratized, and that at best, they are being sufficiently prepared to enable them to earn a good living. But paramountly, they also feel they are not being offered stimulating intellectual food in large enough portions to enhance their sense of aliveness. These students insist that they do not want to be dead in the midst of plenty; they insist that they do not want to study in institutions which, in their yielding to the vested interests of professors, administrators, and governmental forces, pay too little attention to their generation's need for a critical examination of today's conventional wisdom.

The campus rebels, even though sometimes misled through political naivete and lack of realism, and even though sometimes motivated by destructive drives, at least draw attention to the fact that today's processes of higher education are deemed unsatisfactory by a large number of the young element.

The educational failure of our high schools is even worse. By his very action, each drop-out casts a vote against the education he has been receiving. Who would deny that juvenile delinquency is related to the failure of our educational system to provide stimulation and meaning for our adolescents.

The educational system, of course, reflects the social and cultural processes of society as a whole. Unfortunately, the last ten years have not brought about any improvement. The war in Vietnam goes on; consumption increases for the affluent; poverty remains or gets worse, both nationally and internationally.

Our economic system is geared to produce men who fit its needs: men who cooperate smoothly, men who want to consume more and more, men whose tastes are standardized, men who can be easily influenced, men whose needs can be anticipated, and men whose needs can be manipulated.

By the very nature of this process, our system also creates men who are anxious, men who are bored, men who feel inordinately lonely, men who have few convictions, men who have scant values, and most deplorably, men who have no joy in living. For most individuals today experience little aliveness within themselves. Such men often become destructive and violent because the unlived life wants to revenge itself on life, by strangling and destroying life in all its manifestations.

It, therefore, would seem rewarding to examine afresh the goals of *Summerhill,* and to discuss what Summerhill attempts to achieve as against what the existing educational system has actually developed.

What is the root of Neill's system? Is it freedom? What is freedom? Does freedom mean individuality? Does Summerhill connote the absence of deception? Does Neill stand for the absence of authority? The death of conventionality? Self government by children? What?

Many more concepts could be nominated. In searching for a principle from which all these would follow, I have come to conclude that Neill's basic precept is no other than *love of life.*

Summerhill is an expression of *biophilia.* The practical application of Neill's principles is conducive to create a love of life in the young people whom he guides.

What is this love of life? Do we not all love life? Can there be a particular educational system which is characterized by the love of life?

First of all, love of life—I called it *biophilia* in my book *The Heart of Man*—is not shared by all of us even in its simple biological reference, as is demonstrated by the phenomenon of suicide. Granting that suicide is the consequence of an exceptional, pathological condition, the fact that many persons neither love life, nor respect life, is clear.[1] Some individuals who do not respect life do not kill themselves, but maim and kill others. Even the leaders of the most powerful nations on earth are willing to contemplate global destruction (which, of course, might include the destruction of their own country) as a measure which one day might "become necessary."

When I speak of love of life, I am not primarily talking about

[1] See a detailed discussion of this problem in *The Heart of Man* by Erich Fromm, Harper & Row, New York, 1964.

"hanging on to life," nor am I talking about the biologically rooted wish for physical survival. I speak about a certain quality of living which we have in mind when we say about someone: "He really loves life," or when we say: "She is very much alive."

The biophilous person is attracted by the very *process* of life, and by growth of every manner. He prefers to construct, rather than to retain. He is capable of wondering. He prefers to seek something new, rather than to merely confirm the old. He loves the sheer adventure of living, for life always implies uncertainty and risk. His approach is functional, rather than mechanical. He sees the whole rather than its parts. He prefers structure to summation. He wants to mold and influence by stimulation, not by force. He wants to examine things—not to cut them apart—to look for the *why*. He essentially enjoys *life*, not mere excitement.

Biophilia has its own ethic, its own principle of good and evil.[2] Albert Schweitzer has formulated this principle in its most universal form as: "Reverence for life." In biophilic ethics, *good* is all that is conducive to growth and unfolding, while *evil* is all that strangles life, freezes life, and macerates life.

Characteristic expression of biophilic ethics are Spinoza's statements: "Pleasure in itself is not bad but good; contrariwise, pain in itself is bad." (*Ethics, IV,* 41); and "A free man thinks of death least of all things; and his wisdom is a mediation, not of death, but of life." (*Ethics, IV,* 47).

One can understand biophilia fully only by comparing its opposite: *necrophilia.* Necrophilia is the attraction of and the affinity to death, destruction, decay, and sickness. Necrophilia is all that is not alive, the purely mechanical.

[2] See biblical statement that holds lack of joy as a fundamental sin of the Hebrews: "Because thou didst not serve the Lord with joy and with gladness of heart, for the abundance of all things." (Deut. 28:47) Also see Psalms (118:17) "I will not die, but I shall live, and I will relate the deeds of the Lord," the logic being that the dead can pay no reverence to a living force.

The necrophilous person is attracted by all that is against life: he craves for certainty, and hates uncertainty; he hates life which by its own nature is never certain, never predictable, rarely controllable. In order to control life, life must be fragmented, cut into pieces—that is killed! Death, indeed, is the *only* certainty in life. The necrophilous person smells death everywhere. Just as Midas transformed everything he touched into gold,[3] so the necrophilous person is fascinated by all that is not alive. He likes to talk about sickness, death, burials, money, gadgets, and punishment. The necrophilous person is attracted by all that does not grow, by everything that is static, by the purely mechanical. He would transform the organic into the inorganic. He approaches life mechanically and bureaucratically, as if all living persons were merely *things*. He prefers memory to understanding, *having* to *being*. He is attracted only to that which he possesses; hence, a threat to his possessions is a threat to his life. And precisely because he is afraid of life which he can not control, he is attracted to all that is mechanical, to gadgets, and to machines which he *can* control.

It is hardly necessary to stress that contemporary technological civilization encourages this attitude. Our system tends to make people part of the machine, or subparts of the parts—all unified by the self-same program transmitted to every one through the same education, the same radio, the same television, the same magazine.

The question arises: Where are we headed? If we go on losing aliveness, will we not end up as frightened, isolated, unproductive particles, unfit to live and eventually preferring mass suicide to unbearable boredom?

I have talked in some detail about biophilia and necrophilia because I believe that the Summerhill system is rooted in the biophilous principle, that that is why Neill has attracted the inter-

3 Freud has pointed to the symbolic identity: gold equals feces equals dirt.

est and enthusiasm of so many people, and why Summerhill is one of the crucial experiments of our time. For Summerhill. presents the possibility of a life-oriented rather than a death-oriented culture.

Neill's fundamental goal is to bring up children who are *alive*, who are inwardly active individuals rather than passive spectators and consumers. Education for him has only one purpose: *living*. And living has no purpose except—living! To be clever, skilled, brilliant, creative, is all well and good. But these goals should not be primary; they should not be ends in themselves. These goals should not be permitted to *control* life.

What Neill wants to produce is a *good* man. A good man is an alive man, a man in tune with life, in tune with other men, in tune with Nature, in tune with the rhythm that pulses through all existence.

This principle of Summerhill is difficult to understand. Technological society has deeply implanted in us the idea that what matters most are *purposes;* that one lives in order to *achieve;* that position, skill, prestige, money, and security are the great desiderata.

The critics of Summerhill say, in effect, that living just in order to live, just to enhance the quality of living, just to develop greater inner activity—well, that may all be very nice—sort of as a hobby as it were—but certainly not acceptable as a prime goal. Living for just the sake of living without *having*, without any achievement to show for it—that is plainly immoral. Such critics cannot comprehend the Summerhill criterion: not *what* one is, but *who* one is.

Yet even many of those who are puzzled by the apparent aimlessness of Summerhill are strongly attracted by the concept, often even without quite knowing why. I believe the answer lies in the fact that they, themselves, feel their own lack of aliveness and joy. They are dimly aware of their loneliness and anxiety; and they sense the excitement and wonder of life that shines through Neill and all that he touches.

From the fundamental principle *education for being alive,* a number of other principles follow which are quite logically applied in Summerhill. First and foremost, there is the principle of non-lying, or formulated positively, the utter truthfulness of Neill's relationship to the children. It is, indeed, most unusual that it can be said of any man as it can be of Neill that he never lied to a child (although if one listens to the values which are preached in schools and churches that should be most commonplace).

What is the connection between truth and love of life? Untruth and illusions are necessary only to the extent to which life is not fully lived, is strangled or distorted. As long as the unsatisfactory real conditions of life remain such, they will require illusions in order to be tolerable. Man will lie to himself and will lie to others. Contrariwise, the more man transforms his real existence into one conducive to the enhancement of living, the more he can stand the truth.

Man's strength lies in his capacity to know what is real, in order to change that reality in accord with his needs. The greater his knowledge, the greater his strength. As Paracelsus said, "He who knows nothing, loves nothing. He who can do nothing, understands nothing. He who understands nothing is worthless. But he who understands also loves, notices, sees. The more knowledge is inherent in a thing, the greater the love."

On the other hand, only if a person is very much alive can he stand the full truth; the more unalive and ossified he is, the less able is he to bear the truth. For such a man, truth becomes a veritable menace because truth would force him to revisions which he is incapable of making. For the person who is alive, the truth is a challenge to him to give up inadequate positions for the sake of those more valid; and a challenge to actualize his possibilities.

Any person who reacts primarily with an impulse to use force in order to attain what he wants is a person with little love of life. For him everybody is estranged; every other individual is an "object," something dead. And dead things can be moved—not through persuasion—but only through force. Starting on this premise, he is more or less right.

But what holds true of the dead does not hold true of the alive. First of all, all living substance grows at its own pace. A tree needs a given time to grow, its own good time, just as an infant does. He who would use force to change the rhythm of growth would actually destroy the growing thing. Not only is force harmful to growth, but care and knowledge are needed to help growth. One who forgets to water his plants, or one who gives them too much water is like the mother who would feed her infant only when he pleases her by his smile. Such a gardener must control either by smothering over-attention or by neglect; he would kill what he claims he wants to protect.

Love of life has its own way of producing changes: by understanding, by example; and most of all, by changing one's self, rather than by changing everything else except one's self.

The tendency to use violence and force can be rationalized in many ways and usually is—especially by governments who, by definition, enjoy a monopoly on the use of force. One can argue endlessly whether one should use force to save one's life, or freedom, or property, or honor. Such arguments usually get stuck at some fine abstract level; and at that point, no solution can really be found. But the difficulty largely disappears if one ceases to think in terms of casuistic abstract principles, and instead approaches the matter with a total orientation toward life. The life-loving person may *sometimes* use force; he may, or he may not, be able to justify his specific act in terms of general principles. But whether one agrees with or disagrees with that particular action, one knows and recognizes that that individual is, by and large, motivated by a deep love and concern for life.

On the other hand, the necrophilous person may, under certain circumstances, refrain from using force, and yet we know that he is, by and large, motivated by indifference to life or a hatred of life. He might, for instance, passively watch persons being starved to death, because he adheres to a rigid and abstract principle of non-violence. In the question of the use of force, what matters is not so much a single action as the attitude behind that action. If one does not comprehend this, one can easily get into all sorts of silly arguments about the use of force in Neill's system.

If Neill favors not permitting a youngster to interfere with the legitimate interests or activities of others, he will not refrain from using force to remove an intruder bodily from the room. But then, is not any kind of punishment, or even the threat of punishment, a use of force? All such arguments are sophistry and merely serve to becloud the issue. One need not deal with such specious arguments if one understands that the core of the matter lies in one's basic attitude—not in a single isolated act. Neill's life-centered posture is clear for all to see; in it is embedded the root of his principle of no pressure.

The avoidance of force is basic to the principle of freedom for the child. Neill has been criticized for his alleged ultra-permissiveness: any child can do as he pleases without restriction. Nonsense! Those who have criticized Neill in this way have plainly misunderstood him in spite of the fact that he expressed his ideas quite clearly in *Summerhill*.

Many well meaning parents misunderstood Neill and tried to imitate what they *thought* was Neill's concept of freedom. And with very poor results. In fact, so many parents misunderstood

Neill that his publisher implored him to write a book in explanation, saying: "You must, for so many American parents who have
read *Summerhill* feel guilty about the strict way they treated
their child, and tell their child that from now on, he is free. The
result is usually a spoiled brat, for the parents have scant notion
of what freedom is."[4] In consequence, Neill wrote *"Freedom—
Not License!"* from which the above lines are quoted, in which
he included many answers he gave to parents concerned with the
problem of freedom.

In general terms, Neill defines license as interfering with
another's freedom. Thus license becomes antithetical to freedom.
Freedom, on the other hand, implies self-control. By self-control,
Neill does not refer to the Victorian ideal of repression and virtue
but to *"the ability to think of other people,* to respect the rights
of other people."[5]

For Neill, this emphasis on respect and consideration are
essential elements of freedom and not only its limits. I should like
to put the same idea into somewhat different words and to show
the connection between freedom and biophilia. I will begin by
distinguishing two concepts which today are virtually used inter-
changeably: *responsibility* and *duty*. If we say to a man, it is your
duty to pay your taxes, to obey the laws, to take care of your
family, we are in effect saying it is your *responsibility*. But, the
two words—duty and responsibility—are really quite different. In
fact, in a certain sense they are opposites.

The word *duty* comes from the Latin root *deber* which means
to owe. This original meaning is still alive when we speak of
"custom duties," etc. A person who "does his duty" pays what he
owes to the state or to society, or to his parents, that is, to the
authority which controls him. If he does not do his duty, he is

4 A. S. Neill, *Freedom—Not License!* Hart Publishing Co., New York 1966, p.7
5 ibid. p.8 (A. S. Neill's italics)

disobedient and deserves to be punished. What his duty is and what the punishments for transgression should be are determined by the self-same authority.

When a person refuses to pay duties imposed upon him by the authorities, he is rebelling not primarily against *what* he has to pay, but against the *method* by which his duty has been determined. In a narrower or broader sense, he has become a revolutionary. Examples of such rebellion abound in history: refusal to pay the duty on tea was one of the reasons for the American revolution; refusal to pay the British salt tax was one of the main revolutionary symbols used by Gandhi.

On the other hand, responsibility derives from the Latin root *respondere*, to respond. A human being who responds to what is in front of him, is a "responsible" person. What does *to respond* mean? A tree responds to the sun by turning to the light, even if in that process it has to twist itself and grow in an abnormal fashion (abnormal, that is, when measured against the orderly and normal shape it would take had it not to seek for the sun from its peculiar position). A mother responds to a child's smile with her own smile. She responds to the child's cry of hunger by feeding him. The infant responds to the mother's face, eyes, voice and touch. A person responds to the joy or sadness of another. One responds to a painting, to a piece of sculpture, or to music or to an interesting idea. In fact, all living acts are responses by which man expresses his feelings. Man is not only motivated by the need to get rid of inner physiological tensions; he is equally motivated by the need to express what he is able to express. As Marx put it: "Passion is man's faculties striving to attain their object." Because I have eyes, I have the need to see; because I have ears, I have the need to hear; because I have a brain, I have a need to think; because I have a heart, I have a need to feel.

Only the person who is alive can respond; or more correctly, the extent to which a person is alive is the extent to which he responds. To the extent he is unalive, he can *not* respond. "Not the dead shall praise thee, Oh Lord, nor they who descend into the shadows," as the Psalmist expresses it poetically.

From the foregoing a general formulation follows: freedom implies responsibility; responsibility implies the capacity to respond; the capacity to respond implies aliveness.

On the other hand, the necrophilous person—the person with a greatly reduced love of life—can not react responsibly *because he can not respond!* The only principle by which he decides is that of duty; that is, obedience to "law and order." In acting according to this principle, he also satisfies his own passion for control and the exercise of power over others. To put it differently: by doing one's duty, one may negate one's responsibility.

Today, in a civilization in which everything has become a commodity and everybody has become a total consumer, there are two opposite forces which identify freedom with license. There are the adjusted people who merely consume and are scant alive, and who believe that only if we were ruled by law and order, we could avoid anarchy and licentiousness. And then there are many of the young who believe that freedom means absence of tradition, absence of structure, absence of plan: what is desirable is unstructured, spontaneous action. They often believe that "the old ideas" and values are of little or no use today, that to know tradition, not to speak of accepting some of it, is in itself an obstacle to freedom.[6] Their error lies in their confusing *structure* with *order*. I believe that the word *structure* applies to living processes, and that the word *order* applies to mechanical changes.

All life—and all inorganic matter too—implies structure, that is,

---

[6] One can hear this expressed in a very primitive form by many young students; and also expressed in a veiled, highly sophisticated form, in the writings of H. Marcuse.

system. Where structure is destroyed, pathology and death set in. Hence where there is a process of life there must necessarily be structure.

But such structure is radically different from mechanical *order*. It is through *order* that life is cut down to fit the demands of those who are afraid of life and are attracted to death.

Today, the crucial danger in an automatized, gadget-ridden, consumer culture is that we are becoming less and less alive, and more and more alienated from each other and from our very selves.

Neill's principles, I grant, are most difficult to translate into practice by any person who does not possess his great aliveness and his dramatic imagination. Yet his work confronts each of us with the crucial fact that his is an education for biophilia. In his system, the goals are radically different than they are in a system of education which tends to transform man into an instrument of achievement, duty, order, and service to the state.

Neill has the courage to show what results if one takes "living" seriously, and stops gilding his alleged aims. Any critique of Neill's work must fall within this purview. Otherwise, such criticism is a mere hitting out against an educational system whose essence one does not comprehend.

Index